THE NEW SOUTHERN COOKBOOK

The NEW SOUTHERN COOKBOOK

CLASSIC FAMILY RECIPES *and* MODERN TWISTS ON OLD FAVORITES

PAM WATTENBARGER & BRITTANY WATTENBARGER

PHOTOGRAPHY BY HÉLÈNE DUJARDIN

ROCKRIDGE
PRESS

For general information on our other products and services or to obtain technical support, please contact our Customer Care Department within the United States at (866) 744-2665, or outside the United States at (510) 253-0500.

Rockridge Press publishes its books in a variety of electronic and print formats. Some content that appears in print may not be available in electronic books, and vice versa.

TRADEMARKS: Rockridge Press and the Rockridge Press logo are trademarks or registered trademarks of Callisto Media Inc. and/or its affiliates, in the United States and other countries, and may not be used without written permission. All other trademarks are the property of their respective owners. Rockridge Press is not associated with any product or vendor mentioned in this book.

Designers: Alyssa Nassner (cover);
Liz Cosgrove (text)
Editor: Salwa Jabado
Production Editor: Andrew Yackira

Cover photograph © Marija Vidal, 2018; food styling by Cregg Green. Interior photography © Hélène Dujardin, 2018; food styling by Tami Hardeman

ISBN: Print 978-1-64152-173-4 | eBook 978-1-64152-174-1

Thanks to my mom and aunts who taught me Southern cooking. And to our family who eats our cooking.

PAM WATTENBARGER

Thanks to Lynn and Nanny. Sorry about the oven.

BRITTANY WATTENBARGER

CORN BREAD SALAD *page 50*

CONTENTS

A NOTE *from* PAM

Even though I was an only child, I grew up with a huge extended family. My mom was one of 12 children and my dad was one of eight. Our families used any excuse to get together for a meal. This was never a problem for me because they were all good cooks. Some of my favorite memories are centered on those meals.

My mom believed in the philosophy, "We always have room for one more." I never knew if we'd be having a meal with four or 12. Sometimes I thought our neighbor's son had a special radar that could detect when dinner was ready, as he often arrived just as we were setting the table.

As an adult, that philosophy has carried over to my house as well. When the kids were younger, I didn't know how many of their friends would be staying for dinner. I finally started asking, "Are you staying for dinner?" The answer was usually "yes." Most of these friends have moved away, but they still come for dinner when they are in town.

Holidays are still big celebrations at our house. We often host my daughter's friends who don't have family in the area. Their kids even call me "Maymay," just like my granddaughter does. It delighted me then and it delights me now to overhear someone tell Brittany, "I love to eat at your mom's house."

If you're a fan of classic Southern cooking, I share here some of our favorite family recipes—those passed down from my mom, my aunts, and my cousins. Now, for those of you who may not know, traditional Southern cooking is delicious—but fattening, full of butter, and probably fried. In other words, not something you eat every day. Some of our recipes have been updated to make them healthier. Because we have a variety of food allergies at our home, we've included adaptions for gluten-free versions and dairy-free versions when possible. And to accommodate those who follow a vegetarian diet, some dishes are naturally vegetarian, and others include an easy option to convert them. So even if you're not from the South, we hope our recipes will make you want to practice saying "y'all" and plan a visit.

A NOTE *from* BRITTANY

I was born to a long line of home cooks. No matter which family member I had dinner with, the food was always delicious. I worked in gardens alongside my grandparents and parents from an early age, and nothing made me happier than getting to eat the literal fruits of my labor. I was constantly underfoot in the kitchen, oversalting my Goonmomma's mashed potatoes and generally wreaking havoc. If you're wondering about the name, my cousin couldn't pronounce "grand" as a baby, and the names Goonmomma and Goondaddy stuck. They tried to change it, I'm sure, *but it was too late.*

I would like to say that cooking came as naturally to me as it did my relatives, but that would be a lie. In fact, as this book was being written, my grandmother asked my mom if I had ever learned to cook. The answer, obviously, is yes. When I had to cut gluten from my diet, and later dairy from my daughter's, I found myself craving the foods I had grown up with. Since no one else was making them allergy friendly, I set out to do it myself. Mom and I went through a lot of trial-and-error to get it right, but I'm now proficient in both deep-fried, butter-rich cooking and straight from the farmers' market New Southern cooking.

Like my grandparents, mom, and extended family, I always love hearing "company's coming," and my life mission is to fatten up my friends. Nothing makes me happier than coming home from the farmers' market where I work with a cooler full of produce to experiment with.

Here, we've incorporated both our roots and our own food journeys. When you read this cookbook, just imagine pulling up a chair at our table as one of the family. Are y'all hungry? Let's say grace and dig in.

One
MY SOUTHERN KITCHEN

There is nothing that soothes your soul like a plate of Southern cooking. Whether it's piled high with fried green tomatoes, chicken casserole, potato salad, biscuits, corn bread, or something else altogether, Southern food sticks to your ribs. Southern food makes the best of the ingredients that are available and stretches them without seeming stingy. If you're born in the South, Southern cooking will always be part of you. When my friends moved away from our hometown, it's things like sweet tea and good barbecue they miss most. Whether you've grown up with it, married into it, or just plain like it, Southern food is definitely a breed of its own. Recipes are usually passed down without measurements—a Southern recipe box is more like a shopping list: butter, flour, eggs, vanilla. It's written in flowing, neat, yet indecipherable script, or in handwriting that looks like it came from a drunken chicken. Sometimes the written recipe is missing a key ingredient—*that* will only be passed down orally, lest that biddy from church finds out what makes your chicken casserole so special. Southern food is edible history, and once you have sweet tea flowing through your veins, there's just no turning back.

MY RECIPE BOX

PAM Looking through my battered recipe box is a walk down memory lane. It contains recipes I began copying in childhood whenever one of my aunts or cousins made something I liked. I find recipes in my childish scrawl for "baked beans," "fruit pizza," and "hamburger stroganoff." My teenage years brought recipes I learned in home economics, like Angel Biscuits with Sausage Gravy (page 10) and Mississippi mud cake. My adult years include favorites I've picked up from co-workers, people from church, friends, and my in-laws.

After my mother died, her recipe box disappeared. We finally found some of her recipes, and I was instantly transported back to my childhood. She wasn't an adventurous cook and rarely made desserts, but when she did, they were ones that made people beg for the recipes—and a second helping. I can still smell her pound cake, fresh from the oven and cooling on the counter. When she wasn't looking, I'd pinch off a piece and try to pretend some of the cake had just fallen off in the oven. That trick never worked.

Now I'm asked to pass on my recipes to my kids and their friends. Sometimes my son calls from college, asking me to pass along a recipe like my Peanut Butter Sheet Cake (page 152). I gave my daughter my Cranberry Relish (page 17) recipe, and she's passed it along to all of her friends who tell her, "We like this even though we don't like cranberries."

I hope our recipes gathered here bring back treasured memories for you and inspire you to create new ones with your family.

SOUTHERN FOOD TODAY

BRITTANY I lived in St. Louis while away at college, and farm-to-table restaurants were becoming popular. I loved them, but I always found the concept a little confusing. After all, I grew up in a family that would just as soon send me outside to pick some parsley to add to the spaghetti as take a trip to the store. My idea of canned goods included black beans from tin cans and Blue Lake green beans peeking out of the pantry in a Mason jar. I still refuse to eat tomatoes in the winter, a fact that confuses my friends who have grown up with hothouse tomatoes. But here in the South, farm to table isn't just a new trend for restaurants—it's a way of life. I can't get on Facebook without seeing another friend asking what the best freezer is for holding a side of beef they bought from a local farmer. Friends message me weekly, asking which farms are at the farmers' market where I work, and which stand has the best deal on peaches.

Just like farm to table is a merging of the best of farming traditions with modern cooking trends, our family (and most others I know) have kept the best of Southern cooking alive and well in our own kitchens. While we may be just as quick to make pitas as corn bread these days, the essence of Southern cooking lives on.

In this book, we share our tried-and-true heirloom recipes along with some lightened-up, healthier versions. We also share new favorites and allergy-friendly recipes and adaptations. Since we have a whole mess of food allergies in our family, we know just how hard it is to stare at a piece of corn bread, wishing you could eat it like everyone else.

We know we aren't the only people out there combining their family's classic fried chicken recipes with modern, healthier takes on food. We're proud of our gardens, whether 50 acres or a couple of pots on an apartment balcony. We shop local, whether it's a farmers' market in downtown Nashville or a tomato stand near our own farm. We respect the food traditions that came before us, and we're making them our own. We fry green tomatoes with our grandmothers' recipes, and we swap out whole milk for soy milk. Because there's nothing more Southern than making the best food you can with what you've got.

MY SOUTHERN FRIDGE AND PANTRY

PAM Every Southern cook has a list of staples they'd never be without. My family knows there are two items we'll never run out of in our house—toilet paper and my favorite brand of soda—and if we do, it's time for an emergency trip to the store. But I also stock my fridge and pantry with these basic everyday staples that make meal prep run smoothly. One of the easiest ways I know to keep everything on hand is to write a needed item on my shopping list as soon as I see I am running low. This works great, as long as I remember to take my shopping list to the store.

The following items are used frequently in this book's recipes. Write up your list, and soon you'll be on your way to Southern cooking. Just don't leave your shopping list on the fridge!

Buttermilk: This necessary staple keeps in the back of your fridge for weeks and is an absolute must for fried chicken, biscuits, and pancakes. In a pinch, you can make buttermilk using 1 tablespoon of vinegar or freshly squeezed lemon juice mixed with 1 cup of milk. Using high-fat buttermilk, which you can find at small, local dairies, will give baked goods a rich, creamy flavor. If you have leftover buttermilk, freeze it in ice-cube trays and store the frozen cubes in a plastic freezer bag, or freeze the buttermilk in 1-cup containers. Frozen buttermilk is not as creamy as fresh, so it is best used for baking once thawed.

Cooking oil: There's a lot of variety out there, but the most common oils to have on hand are vegetable oil, canola oil, peanut oil, and olive oil. All have high smoke points (the temperature at which the oil starts to break down and burn), making them ideal for frying. Peanut oil has the highest smoke point, at 450°F; next is vegetable oil at 425°F to 450°F; and canola has a smoke point of 400°F. Extra-virgin olive oil has the lowest smoke point, between 325°F and 375°F.

Vegetable oil and peanut oil have the mildest tastes, but once opened, peanut oil needs to be stored in a cool, dark place for no longer than 4 months. A bottle of extra-virgin olive oil is good to have on hand to use for marinades, drizzling, and preparing salad dressings. Additionally, solid coconut oil, stored at room temperature, can be used instead of butter in baked goods.

Cornmeal: Whether you're making a pan of corn bread or going more upscale with polenta, you'll need cornmeal. There are several varieties available, including coarse-ground, medium-ground, fine-ground, and stone-ground. Fine-ground cornmeal is good for batters and corncakes. Medium-ground cornmeal is often used to make a thick, dense corn bread. If you prefer a milder corn bread, use fine-ground cornmeal. Stone-ground cornmeal is produced using traditional methods to enhance the flavor, but it tends to go rancid faster. It can be stored in an airtight container in the refrigerator for up to 4 months.

Grits: What's the difference between grits and cornmeal anyway? Grits and cornmeal are both made from corn but are a world apart. Grits are usually made from ground hominy treated with lye. It makes for a creamier consistency when cooked. There are several types of grits: quick cooking, ready in five minutes or less; instant, which comes in packets; and stone-ground grits, which are slower to cook and are the ones usually found in recipes. Stone-ground grits can be stored in an airtight container in the pantry for up to 1 year, or indefinitely in the freezer.

Flour: This is a must for baking, thickening, or making gravy. All-purpose flour can be stored in an airtight container in the refrigerator or in a cool, dry place in the pantry for up to 2 years, or indefinitely in the freezer. If a recipe calls for self-rising flour, make your own by adding 1½ teaspoons baking powder and ½ teaspoon salt to 1 cup of all-purpose flour.

If you have celiac disease, purchase a bag of gluten-free 1-to-1 baking flour and use it just as you would all-purpose flour in our recipes. We've found it is less expensive than blending our own from several different flours and starches. In places, we also call for gluten-free all-purpose flour and gluten-free baking mix, as some recipes just turn out better with the different ingredients.

Spices and Seasonings: These add flavor to dishes without adding extra calories. A basic spice cabinet should include:

- Black pepper (if possible, get a spice mill and grind your own fresh)
- Cayenne pepper
- Chili powder
- Italian seasoning
- Salt (preferably sea salt)

I also keep bay leaves, oregano, paprika, and parsley (preferably fresh, but dried will work) on hand.

Other ingredients you'll want to have available for baking include:

- Baking powder
- Baking soda
- Ground cinnamon

- Vanilla extract (You can make your own: Add 1 vanilla bean to a pint of vodka and store it in a cool, dark place for 1 month before using.)

Sugar: An essential for baking or preparing the perfect glass of sweet tea, it's good to have all three types of the most common sugars on hand—brown, granulated, and confectioners'. Each will keep indefinitely if stored in an airtight container and kept in a cool, dry location. Sugar can also be frozen indefinitely in an airtight container.

Brown sugar, though, will become hard as a brick if not stored correctly. A simple solution is to place it in a blender or food processor and process for 10 seconds to break up the lumps.

Eggs: You'll use eggs for everything from baking to breakfast. These budget-friendly additions to the fridge can be used in a pinch for dinner, too. Who can resist an omelet? Just fill with chopped leftover meat, onions, peppers, and cheese. Hard-boiled eggs can be made into egg salad or that Southern classic, deviled eggs. You can freeze eggs by breaking the eggs, beating them lightly, and pouring them into ice-cube trays. Freeze until solid. When frozen, place the cubes into freezer-safe containers. The eggs will keep for up to 1 year and can be used for baking, once thawed.

Milk: Used in sauces, baking, and so much more, milk is a must in the fridge.

Many recipes that call for "milk" use *whole milk*. If skim milk is used, it alters the fat content in a recipe, which can make the end result drier. That said, I keep 2% milk in the house unless I have a special dessert or sauce I know needs the flavor. If you don't use milk often, consider purchasing a box of powdered milk for baking. It will keep in the pantry and can be mixed as needed, using 3 tablespoons of dried milk to 1 cup of water.

And, of course, nut or soy milks can be substituted to accommodate allergies or preferences. We do it regularly at our house.

Pasta: This pantry staple can keep for months on the shelf. It's good to have on hand for a quick meal, but it can also be used in soups or stews, pasta salads, and as the basis of casseroles and skillet meals. When adding to soup or skillet meals, wait until the dish is nearly done, and then add the pasta and simmer until the noodles are cooked but still firm. Adding noodles too early soaks up the moisture and results in a drier dish and soggy noodles.

We keep both regular and gluten-free macaroni, spaghetti, and rigatoni in our pantry, along with a jar of pasta sauce.

SUPPORTING EQUIPMENT

PAM I am a sucker for cutesy kitchen gadgets, but you don't have to blow the budget to have all the tools necessary to prepare a meal. Here are some basics we've used in our kitchens for years:

Cast iron skillet: A Southern tradition—once seasoned properly, a cast iron skillet is almost nonstick and can be transferred directly from stove top to oven (and then to table!). It has a variety of uses, from frying and sautéing to baking.

Dutch oven: This multifunctional pot, like your trusty cast iron skillet, can be used in the oven or on the stove top. It distributes heat evenly and is available in several sizes.

Food processor: This tool helps cut prep time—doing everything from chopping and mincing to mixing dough.

Good set of knives: Knives are the backbone of the kitchen. You'll use them for everything from chopping and dicing to slicing and peeling. A basic set should include a chef's knife, paring knife, all-purpose utility knife, and a serrated knife.

Slow cooker: This can be used to prepare anything from main courses to desserts.

With a little advance preparation, it's easy to have a meal waiting when you come home from work, saving time, stress, and money.

ABOUT THE RECIPES

BRITTANY Southerners are a hard-working, straightforward bunch, overall, and we include that Southern sensibility in the way we cook. That means our recipes are good enough for a church potluck but simple enough for a weeknight meal.

Some of the recipes you're about to discover date back to my mom's grandparents' recipe boxes, and they've certainly stood the test of time. These are labeled *Heirloom Recipes*.

We also continue the Southern tradition of cooking with the seasons, using fresh, local ingredients, while modernizing traditional recipes and creating our own new recipes using ingredients we grew up with. Our modern takes on traditional recipes are labeled *Updated Classics,* and our new recipes are labeled *New Favorites.*

Since our family is familiar with food allergies and special diets, we've noted when recipes are dairy free DF, gluten free GF, nut free NF, vegetarian V, and vegan. Some recipes may be easily made gluten or dairy free, or vegan, and we note this in the tips at the bottom of the recipe. **If you need to eat gluten free, remember to check the labels on packages to make sure the food was processed in a gluten-free facility.**

Note that most gluten-free recipes such as breads, muffins, and cakes won't rise as high as regular recipes containing gluten, and dairy-free variations tend to be a little drier than normal because of the different ingredients. *Vegan sour cream just doesn't give the same texture.*

Now that we've covered the basics, it's suppertime, y'all. Come sit a spell and let's eat.

ANGEL BISCUITS WITH SAUSAGE GRAVY *page 10*

Two

BUTTER MY BUTT AND CALL ME A BISCUIT
—
BREAKFAST, BRUNCH, AND BREADS

PAM In the South, we love our carbs. Just about anything can be made into bread or muffins. Fruits, vegetables, nuts, whatever, we find a way to turn it into bread. During visits with the extended family when I was a child, we'd have a big Southern breakfast—complete with platters of biscuits hot from the oven and dripping with butter, bowls of gravy with or without sausage, platters of eggs, and mounds of sausage and bacon. I rarely eat a traditional Southern breakfast now, preferring a muffin I can eat on the run. Sometimes, for a treat, though, I serve these traditional breakfasts to my family for dinner. Even today, when we eat at a meat and three diner I have a hard time deciding between the big bowl of biscuits or corn bread. What's a meat and three? At the meat and three, you choose your meat—probably fried or barbecued—add three Southern veggies—anything from fried okra or macaroni and cheese (*yes, it's a vegetable in the South!*) to banana pudding—and a sweet tea to complete your meal. The recipes in this chapter will remind you of a day at Grandma's, with loving straight from the oven, even if some of the recipes have new twists (such as the gluten-free option included for each recipe in this chapter).

ANGEL BISCUITS WITH SAUSAGE GRAVY

NF | **V**

Heirloom Recipe | MAKES **2** DOZEN BISCUITS

I took every home economics class in high school but enjoyed the cooking classes most. At the beginning of the quarter we were given a budget and a list of dates to make meals, and each meal had to have a theme. This worked well for the first four meals. When it was time for the fifth meal, we had a problem. "When do we get the supplies for our meal?" we queried. "You don't," our teacher said. "You've blown your budgets. You'll have to make a meal using what you can find in the fridge and cabinets." This should have been a challenge, but, hey, we're in the South. "It's breakfast for dinner!" we yelled. Out came the recipes for angel biscuits and sausage gravy, cheesy scrambled eggs, and a breakfast casserole made from stale bread. These biscuits and gravy taste just as good today as they did all those years ago.

FOR THE ANGEL BISCUITS

Nonstick cooking spray

2 tablespoons warm water

1 (¼-ounce) packet dried yeast

5 cups all-purpose flour, plus more for rolling the dough

¼ cup sugar

2 teaspoons baking powder

1 teaspoon salt

1 teaspoon baking soda

1 cup shortening (such as Crisco)

2 cups buttermilk

FOR THE SAUSAGE GRAVY

16 ounces ground pork sausage, hot or mild, crumbled

2 to 4 tablespoons all-purpose flour

2 cups whole or 2% milk

1 teaspoon freshly ground black pepper

PREP TIME: 20 minutes

COOK TIME: 12 to 15 minutes per batch of biscuits, 10 minutes for the gravy

PER SERVING (3 BISCUITS): Calories: 775; Total fat: 43g; Saturated fat: 16g; Cholesterol: 62mg; Carbs: 74g; Fiber: 2g; Protein: 21g; Sodium: 981g

TO MAKE THE ANGEL BISCUITS

1. Preheat the oven to 450°F. Coat a baking sheet with cooking spray, and set it aside.

2. In a cup, combine the warm water and yeast. Stir until dissolved. Let sit for 5 minutes.

3. In a large bowl, stir together the flour, sugar, baking powder, salt, and baking soda.

4. Cut in the shortening until crumbs form (see how-to tip).

5. In a small bowl, stir together the yeast mixture and buttermilk until blended. Add this to the crumb mixture, stirring until a smooth dough forms.

6. Flour a piece of wax paper or a cutting board and transfer the dough to it. Flour your rolling pin and roll out the dough to a ¾- to 1-inch thickness. Use a 2-inch biscuit cutter (or glass) to cut out biscuits. Place the biscuits on the prepared baking sheet. Reroll the scraps and continue cutting biscuits.

7. Bake for 12 to 15 minutes, until golden brown.

TO MAKE THE SAUSAGE GRAVY

1. In a large skillet over medium-high heat, cook the sausage for 5 to 7 minutes or until cooked and no longer pink. With a slotted spoon, transfer the sausage to a paper towel–lined plate to drain, leaving the fat in the pan.

2. Return the skillet to the heat and stir in the flour (depending on how thick you like your gravy, use 2 or 4 tablespoons), cooking and stirring for about 1 minute or until blended.

3. Slowly add the milk to the skillet, stirring continuously until blended.

4. Reduce the heat to low. Simmer for 2 minutes, or until thickened, then remove the gravy from the heat and season with the pepper.

5. Stir in the sausage. Spoon the hot gravy over warm, freshly baked biscuit halves.

HOW-TO TIP: To cut in shortening, add the shortening to the dry ingredients. Use your fingertips to mix the shortening into the dry ingredients until it forms crumbs and the flour is blended with the shortening.

MAKE-AHEAD TIP: Once your biscuits are shaped, wrap them tightly in aluminum foil. Place in an airtight container or freezer bag and freeze until ready to use. Thaw in the refrigerator before baking. Don't need 60 biscuits at once? Make the dough and keep it refrigerated for up to 1 week . . . then just pull out what you need and have fresh-baked biscuits at every meal!

DAIRY-FREE AND VEGAN OPTION: Omit the sausage, use soy or almond milk instead of cow's milk, vegan shortening, and vegan sugar. To replace the buttermilk, combine 1 cup of soy or almond milk with 1 tablespoon of freshly squeezed lemon juice for each cup of buttermilk needed.

GLUTEN-FREE OPTION: Use gluten-free all-purpose flour.

AUNT INEZ'S TURTLE BISCUITS

When we started writing this cookbook, Mom asked what recipes we should put in it. One of my first thoughts was Great-Aunt Inez's biscuits. Inez was a home economics teacher, so when we visited her in Florida, every meal was magical. We had fresh-squeezed orange juice with every meal, and she never failed to make a batch of her biscuits. I looked forward to breakfast every morning, even though I wasn't a breakfast eater. Everything was served family-style, and much of it was fresh from the garden. I would grab a biscuit, split it in half, and pile it high with scrambled eggs, slices of Cheddar cheese, and either jelly or tomato slices. Some of my biscuits would be filled with perfectly cooked bacon or crispy, juicy sausage. Mom clearly remembered those meals with fondness, too, because she agreed to reach out to her cousin to get some of Inez's recipes.

"There's one thing, though," I said. "I just don't know how to shape the biscuits into little turtles."

Mom's jaw just about hit the ground. It turns out, shaping the biscuits into sea turtles is not actually an essential part of Inez's recipe. "She just did that because you were a kid," Mom said. "You don't actually think last time I went to visit she made turtle-shaped biscuits?" Well, the last time I visited Inez I was 18. The biscuits were still turtles. I'm not sure when you grow out of deserving sea turtle biscuits, but it must not be until around 25 or so.

If you're dying to know how she did it, here's her secret, but *don't tell her I told you*: Shape one large biscuit. Divide another biscuit into 5 equal parts and roll each part into a circle. Attach two on each side of the biscuit for the legs. Add one to the top of the biscuit for the head. Add two raisins for eyes. Bake as usual.

—Brittany

BROCCOLI CORN BREAD

NF | **V**

New Favorite | SERVES **8**

When I was about eight, I was at home playing when the phone rang. Mom answered and was surprised to hear the voice of one of our neighbors, who explained that her granddaughter was visiting from New Orleans and staying for a month. She didn't have any friends in town—would Mom be willing to send me over to play with her? Mom packed me up and walked me down the street, where I met my new summer playmate. Like most eight-year-old girls, we loved cartwheels, playing pretend, and climbing trees. We became fast friends and she often asked me to stay for dinner. I almost always agreed, because her grandmother made this amazing broccoli corn bread. When my friend went home at the end of summer, my mom asked our neighbor for the recipe, and we've been making this ever since. Sometimes we substitute a pepper Jack cheese for the Cheddar to give it a flavor twist.

1 cup self-rising cornmeal

½ cup all-purpose flour

2 large eggs, beaten

1 cup buttermilk

8 tablespoons (1 stick) salted butter, melted

1 (10-ounce) package chopped frozen broccoli, thawed

2 cups grated Cheddar cheese

1 small yellow onion, chopped

PREP TIME: 15 minutes

COOK TIME: 25 to 30 minutes

PER SERVING: Calories: 364; Total fat: 23g; Saturated fat: 14g; Cholesterol: 108mg; Carbs: 27g; Fiber: 3g; Protein: 13g; Sodium: 599mg

GLUTEN-FREE OPTION: Substitute gluten-free 1-to-1 baking flour. The corn bread will not rise as much as traditional corn bread but will still taste delicious.

1. Preheat the oven to 350°F.

2. In a large bowl, stir together the cornmeal and flour.

3. Blend in the beaten eggs, buttermilk, and melted butter.

4. Stir in the broccoli, cheese, and onion. Pour the mixture into a medium cast iron skillet.

5. Bake for 25 to 30 minutes, or until a knife inserted into the center comes out clean.

VARIATION TIP: To make basic corn bread, omit 1 egg, the broccoli, cheese, and onion. Mix and bake as directed.

INGREDIENT TIP: Many old recipes call for "sweet milk," which is simply whole milk; you can usually substitute 2% milk with no loss in taste.

SQUASH PUPPIES

One of the first meals I cooked for friends was squash fritters. I was about 10 and had invited Taylor and her mom for dinner. I was so proud of myself as I mixed the batter for fried squash, fried okra, and fried green tomatoes. Unfortunately (for everyone), I had never attempted to fry anything without supervision. In fact, I'm not sure I had attempted to cook *anything* at all without supervision. But this was before I was banned from the kitchen and the minor stove explosion (. . . see Exploding Cupcakes, page 15, for more on that hot mess). *It did not go well, and Mom was madder than a wet hen.*

Years passed—and I was allowed back into the kitchen. After my celiac diagnosis, I learned to excel at cooking. That's when I, once again, attempted a fried squash. This time I was grown up and knew what I was doing—and I had to make them gluten free (see gluten-free option). These squash puppies are good enough to serve to friends and family without worrying they'll never come back. In fact, they might even ask for seconds.

2 tablespoons salted butter

3 or 4 medium yellow squash, sliced

1 medium yellow onion, diced

1 cup self-rising cornmeal

1 cup self-rising flour

1 large egg

1 teaspoon salt

1 teaspoon freshly ground
   black pepper

Peanut oil, for deep-frying

PREP TIME: 20 minutes, plus 10 minutes standing time

COOK TIME: 6 minutes per batch

PER SERVING: Calories: 77; Total fat: 3g; Saturated fat: 1g; Cholesterol: 10mg; Carbs: 11g; Fiber: 1g; Protein: 2g; Sodium: 204mg

1. In a large skillet over medium heat, melt the butter.

2. Add the squash and onion. Cook for about 6 minutes, stirring, until the onion and squash begin to soften. Remove from the heat and mash the squash with a fork. Transfer to a large bowl.

3. To the squash mixture, add the cornmeal, flour, egg, salt, and pepper. Stir just until blended. Let stand for 10 minutes.

4. Add enough peanut oil to fill 3 inches of a Dutch oven. Heat the oil over medium-high heat to 375°F. (Test the temperature with a candy thermometer.)

5. Working in batches, use a tablespoon to carefully drop squash puppies, a few at a time, into the hot oil. Fry for 3 minutes on each side, until crispy and golden brown. Transfer to paper towel–lined plates to drain.

INGREDIENT TIP: These puppies are good with any type of summer or fall squash. Try acorn, butternut, or zucchini.

GLUTEN-FREE OPTION: Use gluten-free 1-to-1 baking flour in place of the self-rising flour.

VEGAN OPTION: Use ¼ cup silken tofu instead of the egg, and vegan butter.

EXPLODING CUPCAKES

When my best friend, Taylor, and I were young, we were determined to learn to cook. We didn't want our parents to help us—we wanted to do it all ourselves. Cupcakes seemed like an easy enough way to start, so we got out our flour, sugar, and the rest of the ingredients. We followed the recipe loosely, *by which I mean not at all*, but everything was going well. We mixed the batter and poured it into the cupcake liners. We put the muffin tin into the oven, and we walked off. I'm not sure what went wrong, but there were cupcakes all over the inside of the oven. It looked like an explosion. I'll never forget when Nanny asked us, "Why is there cupcake on the roof of the oven?" *To this day, we don't have an answer.* Luckily, I have a few cake recipes under my belt now, and we've never re-created this cupcake tragedy.

—*Brittany*

CRANBERRY MUFFINS

V | *New Favorite* | MAKES **1** DOZEN

In fall, when cranberries are abundant and cheap, I stock my freezer so I have enough to make as many batches of cranberry relish as I want during the holidays. This always leaves me with a few extra bags when the holidays are over. Sure, I could save them and make cranberry relish throughout the year, but what makes our relish recipe special is that it's only made during the holidays.

My next-door neighbor, Mary, and I often swap treats. I'll send over some pie, candy, or other sweets, and she'll bring my plate back filled with goodies, like these cranberry muffins. Her motto is, "I don't like to return an empty plate." *Although, sometimes, the treats are intercepted at the door by my son-in-law who eats almost all of them himself.* These moist, yummy muffins are the perfect solution for those extra sacks of frozen cranberries. When you make these, be sure to holler at me. I'll be right over to help you enjoy them.

Nonstick cooking spray

1½ cups cake flour, sifted

1½ teaspoons baking powder

½ teaspoon baking soda

¼ teaspoon salt

6 tablespoons (¾ stick) salted butter, at room temperature

½ cup sugar

1 large egg

¾ cup plain yogurt

1½ teaspoons vanilla extract

1 cup fresh or thawed frozen cranberries, coarsely chopped (or dried cranberries if you haven't stocked up!)

½ cup walnuts, chopped

1. Preheat the oven to 400°F. Coat a 12-cup muffin tin with cooking spray, and set it aside.

2. In a large bowl, stir together the cake flour, baking powder, baking soda, and salt.

3. In a small bowl, using a handheld electric mixer, cream the butter and sugar until blended.

4. Add the egg to the butter mixture and beat until smooth.

5. Add the butter mixture to the flour mixture and beat to combine.

6. Stir in the yogurt and vanilla.

PREP TIME: 15 minutes

COOK TIME: 15 minutes

PER SERVING (1 MUFFIN): Calories: 172; Total fat: 7g; Saturated fat: 4g; Cholesterol: 32mg; Carbs: 23g; Fiber: 1g; Protein: 3g; Sodium: 161mg

7. Fold in the cranberries and walnuts, just until evenly incorporated. Pour the mixture into the prepared muffin tin. Bake for 12 to 15 minutes or until a knife inserted into the center of a muffin comes out clean.

DID YOU KNOW?: Cranberries are native to North America and were once used to dye fabric and cure meat, and to heal wounds.

VARIATION TIP: If you want to shake things up, stir 1 tablespoon dark rum and ⅛ teaspoon ground allspice into the mix.

DAIRY-FREE AND VEGAN OPTION: Substitute vegan butter, use ¼ cup silken tofu instead of the egg, and use soy or coconut yogurt and vegan sugar.

GLUTEN-FREE OPTION: Use gluten-free baking mix instead of flour.

MY MOTHER'S CRANBERRY RELISH

My mom found this recipe on the back of a bag of cranberries and faithfully made it every year for Thanksgiving. When she died, I took over the tradition of making it for our family. After Brittany got married and began hosting a Friendsgiving celebration the day after Thanksgiving, she asked for the recipe. I was in a hurry that day, but wrote it down quickly for her. Two years later, she told me how much her friends loved the recipe and how many people had asked for it. "I told them it was so good because it calls for the same amount of sugar as cranberries." She was expounding on her changes ("Sometimes I use two oranges instead of one . . .") when I exclaimed, "Wait! What are you talking about? No, it doesn't." I had written the recipe incorrectly, listing one package (or 2 cups) of cranberries as 1 cup. "Huh," she said, "that's the recipe I've shared with my friends. They all make it that way now." So, to all Brittany's friends with the wrong recipe, I apologize.

If you, too, want to make it the wrong way, here's the recipe.

1 cup whole cranberries
1 cup sugar
1 orange, peeled and chopped
   into sections

In a food processor fitted with the standard blade, combine the cranberries, sugar, and orange. Process for about 15 seconds, until everything is finely chopped.

—*Pam*

SWEET POTATO MUFFINS

New Favorite | MAKES **1** DOZEN LARGE OR **18** MEDIUM MUFFINS

I will never forget the time one of my close friends, Jen, tried a Southern sweet potato recipe—all gooey and sweet, filled with brown sugar and butter and topped with marshmallows and pecans. Jen is from Brazil, so once in a while I get to introduce her to a uniquely Southern tradition. Some she likes better than others. Sweet potatoes, Southern-style, turned out to be a bit of a culture shock. These sweet potato muffins were our compromise. They're the perfect bridge between sweet potatoes, *the Brazilian way,* and sweet potatoes, *the Georgia way*. I like to serve these with extra butter to spread on the muffins.

Nonstick cooking spray
8 tablespoons (1 stick) salted butter,
    at room temperature
1¼ cups sugar
1½ cups all-purpose flour
2 teaspoons baking powder
1 teaspoon ground cinnamon
¼ teaspoon ground nutmeg
1¼ cups mashed cooked
    sweet potatoes
1 cup whole or 2% milk
½ cup raisins
¼ cup chopped pecans

PREP TIME: 15 minutes

COOK TIME: 25 minutes

PER SERVING: Calories: 259; Total fat: 10g; Saturated fat: 6g; Cholesterol: 26mg; Carbs: 42g; Fiber: 1g; Protein: 3g; Sodium: 87mg

1. Preheat the oven to 400°F. Coat a 12-cup large muffin tin with cooking spray, and set it aside.

2. In a large bowl, use a handheld electric mixer to cream together the butter and sugar until blended.

3. In a medium bowl, stir together the flour, baking powder, cinnamon, and nutmeg.

4. Add the flour mixture to the butter mixture and stir to combine.

5. In a small bowl, stir together the mashed sweet potatoes and milk. Add this to the batter and stir until the ingredients are evenly moistened and blended.

6. Fold in the raisins and pecans. Pour the batter into the muffin tins and bake for 25 minutes or until a knife inserted into the center of a muffin comes out clean. Remove from the oven and place on a wire rack to cool.

HOW-TO TIP: To make all the muffins the same size, use an ice cream scoop to measure the batter. One scoop should fill each muffin cup about two-thirds full.

VARIATION TIP: To give these a twist, add 1 tablespoon bourbon to the batter.

DAIRY-FREE AND VEGAN OPTION: Use soy or almond milk and margarine instead of cow's milk and butter, and vegan sugar.

GLUTEN-FREE OPTION: Substitute gluten-free baking mix for the all-purpose flour.

"MY UNCLE REDDING, WHO LIVED TO BE A HUNDRED, ATE A SWEET POTATO EVERY DAY OF HIS LIFE AND MADE SURE EVERYBODY HE MET KNEW IT."

—VIVIAN HOWARD

PECAN PIE MUFFINS

V | *Updated Classic* | MAKES **1** DOZEN

Some people, such as Miss Eulene, are born cooks. When the kids were younger, she was the neighbor who invited them over to swim in her pool. I'd sit outside on the patio watching over the kids and try to catch whiffs of the aromas drifting from her kitchen. I was never happier than when she would come outside with a plate full of whatever she'd been baking for taste testing. *And she was always baking something.*

At church dinners, the kids would search the tables to find her dishes so they could be first in line to get a spoonful. You had to be quick, because her dishes disappeared before everyone made it through the line. Her pecan pie muffins are one of my favorite snacks, because they have all that pecan pie flavor with less guilt. To make them extra fancy, place a pecan half on top before baking.

Nonstick cooking spray
1 cup packed light brown sugar
½ cup all-purpose flour
2 large eggs
⅔ cup melted salted butter
1 tablespoon pecan bourbon (optional)
1 cup chopped pecans

PREP TIME: 15 minutes

COOK TIME: 15 minutes

PER SERVING: Calories: 209; Total fat: 13g; Saturated fat: 7g; Cholesterol: 58mg; Carbs: 22g; Fiber: 0g; Protein: 2g; Sodium: 90mg

DAIRY-FREE AND VEGAN OPTION: Substitute vegan butter for the dairy butter, ½ cup silken tofu for the eggs, and vegan sugar.

1. Preheat the oven to 350°F. Coat a 12-cup muffin tin with cooking spray, and set it aside.

2. In a large bowl, stir together the brown sugar, flour, eggs, melted butter, and bourbon (if using) just until blended.

3. Stir in the pecans. Pour the batter into the prepared muffin tin, filling each cup two-thirds full.

4. Bake for 12 to 15 minutes or until a knife inserted into the center of a muffin comes out clean.

INGREDIENT TIP: When buying in-shell pecans, look for smooth, light brown shells and uniformity in size and color.

GLUTEN-FREE OPTION: Substitute gluten-free baking mix for the flour.

BACON AND CHEDDAR MUFFINS

Updated Classic | MAKES ABOUT **18**

When the kids were younger, they did not like breakfast. They wanted to sleep until the last minute before being dragged out of bed to go to school. I had to tempt my children to eat. They both liked bacon and cheese, so these muffins were the perfect solution—made ahead, warmed the next morning, and eaten on the way to school. The kids got those extra minutes of sleep, and I got them to eat breakfast. Win-win!

Nonstick cooking spray
3 cups all-purpose flour
½ cup sugar
2 tablespoons baking powder
¼ teaspoon salt
2 large eggs
1½ cups whole or 2% milk
¼ cup vegetable oil
8 bacon slices, cooked and crumbled
¾ cup shredded Cheddar cheese

PREP TIME: 20 minutes

COOK TIME: 20 minutes

PER SERVING (1 MUFFIN): Calories: 208; Total fat: 9g; Saturated fat: 3g; Cholesterol: 37mg; Carbs: 24g; Fiber: 1g; Protein: 8g; Sodium: 275mg

GLUTEN-FREE OPTION: Use gluten-free baking mix.

VARIATION TIP: Don't be afraid to shake things up—use turkey bacon and low-fat pepper Jack cheese to make these muffins a little lighter.

1. Preheat the oven to 400°F. Coat two 12-cup or three 6-cup muffin tins with cooking spray, and set them aside.

2. In a large bowl, stir together the flour, sugar, baking powder, and salt.

3. Add the eggs, milk, and vegetable oil. Using a handheld electric mixer, mix just until combined.

4. Fold in the bacon and cheese. Pour the batter into the prepared muffin tins.

5. Bake for 20 minutes or until a knife inserted into the center of a muffin comes out clean.

MAKE-AHEAD TIP: The batter can be made without the bacon and cheese and frozen in an airtight container until ready to use. Thaw in the refrigerator, then add the bacon and cheese and bake as directed.

HAM BREAKFAST CASSEROLE

NF | *New Favorite* | SERVES **12**

Our major family holidays—Thanksgiving, Christmas, and Easter—are celebrated with ham for dinner. Long ago Bryan told me he had no desire to have turkey at his holiday meals, so ham became our meat of choice. But even with friends and relatives visiting, an 18-pound bone-in ham creates *a lot* of leftovers. We have ham in various dishes for days before everyone says "uncle!" I'm talking ham omelets, ham casserole, pinto beans with ham, ham smoothies—okay, maybe not smoothies. But my family probably expects something that weird one day. After several ham-filled meals, I dice up any leftovers and freeze them.

One day I needed a brunch dish. Usually this isn't a problem, but I hadn't been to the store. I began pulling leftovers and various ingredients out of the fridge, mixing them together to make this breakfast casserole. I knew it was a winner when Bryan said, "This is really good. Could you make this again soon?" Now this is my "go-to" crowd-pleasing dish whenever I have leftover ham.

Nonstick cooking spray
12 slices white bread
12 medium eggs
¾ cup whole or 2% milk
1 teaspoon salt
½ teaspoon freshly ground black pepper
1 to 2 tablespoons salted butter
1 large green bell pepper, diced
1 large yellow onion, diced
1 tablespoon minced garlic
2 cups diced cooked ham
1½ cups shredded Cheddar cheese

PREP TIME: 20 minutes

COOK TIME: 25 to 30 minutes

PER SERVING: Calories: 262; Total fat: 13g; Saturated fat: 6g; Cholesterol: 195mg; Carbs: 20g; Fiber: 1g; Protein: 16g; Sodium: 856mg

1. Preheat the oven to 350°F. Lightly coat a 9-by-13-inch baking pan with cooking spray.

2. Cover the bottom of the prepared pan with the bread slices.

3. In a large bowl, whisk the eggs, milk, salt, and pepper. Set aside.

4. In a medium skillet over medium-high heat, melt the butter.

5. Add the bell pepper and onion. Sauté for 3 to 5 minutes, stirring often.

6. Add the garlic. Sauté for 1 to 2 minutes more or until the vegetables are tender.

7. Stir the vegetable mixture into the egg mixture.

8. Add the ham and cheese and stir to combine. Pour the egg mixture evenly over the bread.

9. Bake for 25 to 30 minutes or until set.

DAIRY-FREE OPTION: Use soy milk and vegan butter and substitute vegan cheese for the Cheddar. We really like the Follow Your Heart brand.

GLUTEN-FREE OPTION: Use gluten-free sandwich bread.

CARROT BREAD

Updated Classic | MAKES **1** LOAF

My Goondaddy loved sweets. His favorite, though, was carrot cake and carrot bread, which we created by adapting our traditional zucchini bread recipe. He'd have us cut him a thick slice and top it with ice cream. When you asked how much ice cream, he'd hold his hands about a foot apart and say, "This much." Then when you gave him the ice cream, he would tell you that you'd given him too much. It turns out most people can't eat a foot of ice cream, but let me tell you, he gave it his best shot. We still can't eat this carrot bread without laughing about Goondaddy and his ice cream demands. I think it's just fine without any extra sweetness, but if you want to try it the Goondaddy way, then you go right ahead.

Nonstick cooking spray

2 cups all-purpose flour, plus more for dusting the pan

1½ cups sugar

2 teaspoons baking soda

2 teaspoons ground cinnamon

½ teaspoon salt

3 large eggs, beaten

1 cup vegetable oil

1 teaspoon vanilla extract

4 or 5 carrots, finely grated

½ cup shredded coconut

½ cup raisins

¼ cup chopped pecans

PREP TIME: 20 minutes

COOK TIME: 1 hour

PER SERVING: Calories: 386; Total fat: 21g; Saturated fat: 2g; Cholesterol: 47mg; Carbs: 48g; Fiber: 2g; Protein: 4g; Sodium: 340mg

1. Preheat the oven to 350°F. Coat a 9-by-5-inch loaf pan with cooking spray and dust it lightly with flour, knocking out the excess. Set aside.

2. In a medium bowl, stir together the flour, sugar, baking soda, cinnamon, and salt.

3. In a large bowl, use a handheld electric mixer to mix the eggs, oil, and vanilla until blended.

4. Add the flour mixture and stir just until blended (see how-to tip).

5. Fold in the carrots, coconut, raisins, and pecans (see ingredient tip). Pour the batter into the prepared loaf pan.

6. Bake for 1 hour or until a knife inserted into the center comes out clean. Let cool partially in the pan and then turn it out onto a wire rack to cool completely before slicing.

HOW-TO TIP: Don't overmix quick bread batter or the bread will be tough. Stir the ingredients together just until combined.

INGREDIENT TIP: To keep ingredients like raisins from sinking to the bottom of the bread, lightly coat them with flour before adding them to the dough.

GLUTEN-FREE OPTION: Use gluten-free baking mix instead of flour.

VEGAN OPTION: Use 1½ cups silken tofu instead of the eggs, and vegan sugar.

LEMON-ORANGE TEA BREAD

NF | **V**

Updated Classic | MAKES **1** LOAF

My best friend, Taylor, loves sweet tea. She recently moved to Colorado, and I get at least a text a week about how sad it is to live somewhere where the tea is unsweet. When she returns to the area, the one thing she really wants is to sit down with a big glass of sweet tea, preferably on a nice porch somewhere. *But you can't just have a glass of sweet tea.* You need something to go with it. This lemon-orange tea bread is perfect for pairing with a little sweet tea (with fresh-squeezed lemon in it, of course). The orange and lemony flavor is refreshing on a hot summer day, but its richness is perfect for filling a little hungry spot. I updated this so all my vegan friends can enjoy it, too! (See the dairy-free and vegan option.) If you're like me—and Taylor— you probably can't have just one piece of this bread. If you're gonna go to the trouble of cutting yourself a slice, you might as well have two.

FOR THE BREAD

Nonstick cooking spray

2 cups cake flour, plus more for
    dusting the pan

8 tablespoons (1 stick) salted butter,
    at room temperature

1 cup sugar

1 cup sour cream

1 tablespoon grated lemon zest

1 teaspoon baking soda

⅛ teaspoon salt

FOR THE GLAZE

½ cup sugar

2 tablespoons freshly squeezed
    orange juice

PREP TIME: 20 minutes

COOK TIME: 50 minutes

PER SERVING: Calories: 312; Total fat: 12g;
Saturated fat: 7g; Cholesterol: 29mg; Carbs: 42g;
Fiber: 1g; Protein: 3g; Sodium: 363mg

TO MAKE THE BREAD

1. Preheat the oven to 350°F. Coat a 9-by-5-inch loaf pan with cooking spray and dust it lightly with flour, knocking out the excess. Set aside.

2. In a large bowl, use a handheld electric mixer to cream the butter and sugar until blended.

3. Stir in the sour cream and lemon zest until blended.

4. Sift the cake flour into a medium bowl.

5. Stir the baking soda and salt into the flour. Slowly mix the flour mixture into the butter mixture. Pour the batter into the prepared loaf pan.

6. Bake for 50 minutes or until a knife inserted into the center comes out clean.

TO MAKE THE GLAZE

1. In a small bowl, combine the sugar and lemon juice. Stir until combined.

2. Pour the glaze over the hot bread. Let the bread sit for 10 minutes before removing it from the pan to cool completely.

HOW-TO TIP: If you use a glass pan for baking, reduce the oven temperature to 325°F.

DAIRY-FREE AND VEGAN OPTION: Substitute vegan butter, vegan sugar, and vegan sour cream.

GLUTEN-FREE OPTION: Substitute gluten-free baking mix (we like Pamela's brand).

"WHEN LIFE GIVES YOU LEMONS, STICK THEM IN YOUR SWEET TEA."

—SOUTHERN SAYING

BLUE CHEESE AND BACON DEVILED EGGS *page 31*

Three

—

APPETIZERS AND SNACKS

BRITTANY If you're having a get-together, you have to have food. I didn't make this rule of Southern hospitality, but I'm more than happy to follow it. Whether you call them snacks, appetizers, hors d'oeuvres, small plates, mezzes, or tapas, I'll gladly whip some up for any occasion. In fact, there doesn't even have to be an occasion! My favorite summer Saturdays are those when we pack the car with a cooler full of snacks and hit the road for an impromptu picnic. We've spent many happy weekends on the banks of the Tennessee River, eating fruit and appetizers and dipping our toes in the water. Having a favorite chapter of this book is a bit like having to choose a favorite child, but if I had to pick, it would be this one. Skip the fuss next time you're planning a big family dinner, and throw some burgers on the grill while you put together some of these recipes. And, to make life easier, we've adapted some recipes so they're easier to prepare, giving you more time to sit on the riverbank and enjoy life.

BACON PIMENTO CHEESE

GF | **NF** | *Updated Classic* | MAKES **2 ½** CUPS

If you want good classic Southern cooking, the best place to find it is at a church dinner. The home cooks are always ready and willing to whip up casseroles or desserts. Their motto is, "If you leave hungry, it's nobody's fault but your own."

My friend Cristal is well known at our church dinners for her scrumptious recipes, like this bacon pimento cheese. Thankfully, she graciously shares her recipes and never leaves out those one or two essential ingredients—like some people I know. *Y'all, that's just mean.*

The secret of a good pimento cheese recipe is the Cheddar. It has to be sharp or the recipe won't have enough zing. Use this pimento cheese filling, with some bacon to give it extra oomph, in your next grilled cheese, and you'll never go back to basic grilled cheese again.

2 cups shredded sharp
    Cheddar cheese
1 (4-ounce) jar diced pimentos, rinsed
    and drained
½ cup mayonnaise
2 tablespoons diced onion
1 tablespoon Worcestershire sauce
¼ teaspoon salt
⅛ teaspoon cayenne pepper
⅛ teaspoon freshly ground
    black pepper
4 bacon slices, cooked and crumbled

PREP TIME: 20 to 25 minutes

PER SERVING (¼ CUP): Calories: 196; Total fat: 15g; Saturated fat: 6g; Cholesterol: 35mg; Carbs: 7g; Fiber: 1g; Protein: 9g; Sodium: 475mg

1. In a medium bowl, combine the cheese, pimentos, mayonnaise, onion, Worcestershire sauce, salt, cayenne, and black pepper. Stir until just blended.

2. Add the crumbled bacon and stir well. Refrigerate in an airtight container for up to 1 week.

DID YOU KNOW?: The phrase "bringing home the bacon" was likely first used in twelfth-century England. One story says a side of bacon was offered by a church in Dunmow, England, to any man who would swear he had not quarreled with his wife for one year and a day.

INGREDIENT TIP: If shredding your own cheese, 4 ounces of block cheese, shredded, equals 1 cup.

BLUE CHEESE AND BACON DEVILED EGGS

GF | **NF**

Updated Classic | MAKES **24**

It's not a holiday around here unless there are deviled eggs. If you're lucky, or if you're a Baptist, there are usually several types of deviled eggs on the buffet. Some are plain. Some are sprinkled with paprika. Some have pickles, sweet relish, or shredded carrots added. Ever since I was a kid, I've been considered a deviled egg expert. I looked forward to church potlucks and family gatherings for many reasons, but there were two things I thought a meal wasn't complete without: sweet tea and deviled eggs.

When Mom came up with this recipe, I warned her not to get crazy with perfection. "Just try it," she said. It was an effective argument. These blue cheese and bacon deviled eggs are some of the best I've ever had, and we've had them at countless family gatherings since. If we haven't served them at church, well, it's only because I don't like to share.

12 hard-boiled eggs, peeled and halved lengthwise

¼ cup blue cheese dressing

1 tablespoon prepared yellow mustard

½ teaspoon salt

½ teaspoon freshly ground black pepper

1 cup crumbled cooked bacon, plus more for garnishing (optional)

½ cup crumbled blue cheese

½ cup chopped onion

1. Remove the egg yolks and place them in a large bowl. Reserve the whites.

2. Add the blue cheese dressing and mustard to the yolks. Stir everything until blended.

3. Stir in the salt and pepper.

4. Add the bacon, blue cheese, and onion. Stir until blended. Spoon 1 to 2 tablespoons of filling into each egg white half.

5. Sprinkle with additional bacon crumbles (if using). Refrigerate until ready to serve (or eat immediately!).

PREP TIME: 15 minutes

PER SERVING (2 HALVES): Calories: 223; Total fat: 17g; Saturated fat: 6g; Cholesterol: 212mg; Carbs: 2g; Fiber: 1g; Protein: 15g; Sodium: 744mg

INGREDIENT TIP: Hard-boiled eggs will keep in the refrigerator for 1 week.

HOW-TO TIP: To make the eggs easier to peel, place them in a bowl of ice water. Gently tap the eggs against the side of the bowl to crack the shell. Peel the egg under the water.

BLACK BEAN DIP

DF | **GF** | **NF** | **Vegan**

New Favorite | MAKES **2** CUPS

We love black beans, but we rarely ate them until we discovered my daughter's food allergies and had to make drastic changes in our diet. Now, my daughter, who is only two, thinks no meal is complete without black beans. It doesn't matter what form they come in: plain, refried, bean salad, chili, or bean dip. When summer comes around and hot food sounds unappealing, this black bean dip is the perfect thing to have on hand. I don't have to fire up the stove when it's a hundred and ten outside, and Jenna is still happy there are black beans available. This is perfect for cookouts, tailgates, and church potlucks that you forgot about until you're about to go to bed on Saturday evening. *Not that I'm speaking from experience!* This black bean dip does well with veggies, and you can't go wrong with tortilla chips.

2 garlic cloves

1 (15-ounce) can black beans, rinsed and drained

2 tablespoons freshly squeezed lemon juice

¼ cup olive oil

2 tablespoons fresh cilantro leaves

1½ teaspoons ground cumin

1 teaspoon cayenne pepper, or to taste

½ teaspoon salt

PREP TIME: 10 minutes, plus 2 hours chilling time

PER SERVING (¼ CUP): Calories: 115; Total fat: 7g; Saturated fat: 1g; Cholesterol: 0mg; Carbs: 11g; Fiber: 4g; Protein: 4g; Sodium: 148mg

1. In a food processor fitted with the standard blade, process the garlic until minced.

2. Add the black beans and lemon juice. Process until smooth.

3. Add the olive oil, cilantro, cumin, cayenne, and salt. Process until smooth. Refrigerate for 2 hours before serving for the flavors to blend.

INGREDIENT TIP: Freshly cooked beans can be frozen for up to 6 months if stored in an airtight bag or container. Let the beans cool thoroughly before placing them in the bag. Unpeeled garlic bulbs can be stored for up to 4 months in a cool, dark cabinet or pantry.

HONEY GRILLED PEACHES

DF | GF | NF | V

New Favorite | SERVES **4** TO **8**

Last year, while working for Humble Heart Farm at the farmers' market, our booth was beside a fruit stand. What fruits they sold changed depending on the season. In June, they had peaches. Behind the scenes at the farmers' market is a lively bartering economy. My goat cheese for your bread. Your green beans for our Cheddar. And, one day, our goat cheese for a bag of peaches. My boss asked if I liked peaches. "My daughter loves them," I said. Without any ceremony, the bag of peaches was plopped into the cooler I take home with me. They were juicy, perfectly ripe, and there were too many to eat plain before they got overripe. We ate them in smoothies, salads, and raw. And before the bag was finished, our recipe experiments produced these honey grilled peaches. They quickly became a family favorite.

4 medium peaches, halved lengthwise
    and pitted
¼ to ½ cup honey
3 tablespoons packed light
    brown sugar
Vanilla ice cream, for serving
    (optional)

PREP TIME: 5 minutes

COOK TIME: 10 minutes

PER SERVING: Calories: 227; Total fat: 0g; Saturated fat: 0g; Cholesterol: 0mg; Carbs: 59g; Fiber: 2g; Protein: 2g; Sodium: 5mg

DID YOU KNOW?: Peaches were first brought to the coastal Georgia islands of St. Simons and Cumberland by Franciscan monks in 1571. The rest, as they say, is history.

1. Preheat the grill to high heat.

2. Brush the cut sides of the peaches with honey and place them cut-side down on the grill. Cook for 4 to 5 minutes. Turn the peaches over and cook for 4 to 5 minutes more, or until tender.

3. Remove the peaches from the grill and sprinkle the brown sugar evenly over them. Serve with a scoop of ice cream (if using).

VARIATION TIP: If you don't have a grill or it's not grilling season, preheat the broiler. Place the peaches cut-side up on a baking sheet. Drizzle with honey and sprinkle with the brown sugar. Let sit for 5 to 10 minutes. Broil for 6 to 8 minutes or until tender.

CLASSIC CHEESE BALL

GF | **V** | *Heirloom Recipe* | MAKES **16** SNACK-SIZE SERVINGS

When I was pregnant with my son, Ashton, I craved cheese. Not just any kind of cheese, mind you; I wanted the fancy stuff from the gourmet section. When Bryan opened the fridge he would ask, "Is cheese all we have?" *Yes. Don't get in the way of the cravings of a pregnant woman!*

Apparently, the love of cheese can be passed down, because my son is also a cheese connoisseur. Once, when visiting a dairy that specialized in gourmet cheese, he sampled the varieties and picked out a package for himself. As we drove away he piped up from the back seat, "I've got cheese and peach Nehi soda. I have everything I need to be happy!" I have a soft spot for this cheese ball because my mom used to make it. It's what first started my love of cheese. It's also easy to update: just substitute your favorite cheese and experiment to find the perfect flavor combination. I recommend blue cheese as a substitute for the Parmesan.

1 pound extra-sharp Cheddar cheese, grated

1 (8-ounce) package cream cheese, at room temperature

1 to 2 tablespoons diced onion

1 tablespoon grated Parmesan cheese

1 tablespoon chopped fresh chives

1 tablespoon mayonnaise

½ teaspoon paprika

1 cup chopped pecans

Salted butter or nonstick cooking spray, for greasing your hands

Gluten-free crackers, for serving

1. In a large bowl, use a handheld electric mixer to blend the Cheddar cheese and cream cheese until smooth.

2. Add the onion, Parmesan cheese, chives, mayonnaise, and paprika. Mix well.

3. Place the pecans in a shallow bowl.

4. Grease your hands with some butter and shape the cheese mixture into a ball. Roll the cheese ball in the pecans until coated. Refrigerate for at least 1 hour before serving. Place on a serving plate and surround with gluten-free crackers.

PREP TIME: 20 minutes, plus 1 hour chilling time

PER SERVING: Calories: 189; Total fat: 17g; Saturated fat: 10g; Cholesterol: 48mg; Carbs: 1g; Fiber: 0g; Protein: 9g; Sodium: 234mg

HOW-TO TIP: Store cheeses properly, and they will stay fresh longer. Before refrigerating, cover soft cheeses tightly with plastic wrap, and wrap hard cheeses in wax paper.

INGREDIENT TIP: Substitute Colby Jack or pepper Jack for the sharp Cheddar cheese.

VEGAN OPTION: Use vegan cheeses and vegan mayo.

"A SHARED RECIPE IN THE SOUTH IS MORE PRECIOUS THAN GOLD . . . AND IT ALWAYS COMES WITH A STORY."

—SOUTHERN SAYING

VIDALIA ONION DIP

GF | NF | V   *Updated Classic* | MAKES ABOUT **4** CUPS

I had never attended college football tailgating parties until my son began attending Mississippi State University. Attending an SEC game tailgate party is serious business, and you quickly see why the unofficial slogan of the South is, "God, sweet tea, and the SEC." Tents are spread all over campus, creating a sea of maroon and white. Everyone stops by the alumni tent to pick up pom-poms and game day stickers. And dressing for the game is a maroon extravaganza—everything from sorority girls wearing cute dresses and stilettos to the casual Go Bulldogs! shirt. Even the babies get into the act. Jenna, my grandbaby, wearing a mini MSU football dress, attended her first tailgating party at the ripe old age of 5 months. No one skimps on food, either, bringing their best goodies. This Vidalia onion dip should earn a place in the (as of yet nonexistent) MSU Hall of Tailgating Fame.

2 large Vidalia or sweet yellow onions, diced
2 (8-ounce) packages cream cheese, at room temperature
2 cups grated Parmesan cheese
⅓ cup mayonnaise
Gluten-free crackers or cut assorted veggies, for dipping

PREP TIME: 15 minutes

COOK TIME: 15 to 20 minutes

PER SERVING (¼ CUP): Calories: 171; Total fat: 15g; Saturated fat: 9g; Cholesterol: 42mg; Carbs: 4g; Fiber: 0g; Protein: 7g; Sodium: 250mg

DID YOU KNOW?: The Vidalia Onion Act of 1986 decreed that only onions grown in certain counties of Georgia could be called Vidalia onions.

1. Preheat the oven to 425°F.

2. In a medium bowl, blend together the onions, cream cheese, Parmesan cheese, and mayonnaise. Spread the dip into a 2-quart casserole dish.

3. Bake for 15 to 20 minutes or until golden brown. Serve with gluten-free crackers or veggies for dipping.

INGREDIENT TIP: To enhance the flavor of cheese in dishes, always bring it to room temperature before use.

VARIATION TIP: To give it a flavor twist, use shredded mozzarella or Gouda instead of Parmesan.

VEGAN OPTION: Use vegan cream cheese, vegan Parmesan cheese, and vegan mayonnaise.

CORN RELISH

DF | GF | NF | V

Updated Classic | SERVES **4**

One of my most unusual experiences with corn happened at a Luke Bryan concert. It was the Farm Tour—in a cleared field surrounded by acres of cornfields—and things seemed to go wrong from the start. There was a mix-up on where to park, followed by a mix-up on our tickets and entry. When the weather unexpectedly turned chilly, my friends and I gave up. We went back to our bus and grabbed some blankets, wraps, a bottle of wine, and snacks. We listened to the concert from a distance, watching people slip in and out of the nearby cornfields. We didn't see the concert from the VIP seating as planned, but we made memories we still laugh about. Whenever I eat corn relish, I'm reminded of that breezy fall evening spent with friends. I like to add a touch of cilantro to update this classic recipe, but you can omit it if you prefer.

FOR THE RELISH

1 (15-ounce) can whole-kernel
    corn, drained, or fresh corn
    (see ingredient tip)
½ (2-ounce) can diced
    pimentos, drained
½ green bell pepper, diced
1 small yellow onion, diced
1 celery stalk, leaves removed, diced
Fresh cilantro, for garnishing (optional)

FOR THE DRESSING

¼ cup sugar
¼ cup vegetable oil
¼ cup white vinegar
½ teaspoon salt
¼ teaspoon freshly ground
    black pepper

Continued

PREP TIME: 10 minutes

COOK TIME: 5 minutes

PER SERVING: Calories: 250; Total fat: 15g;
Saturated fat: 3g; Cholesterol: 0mg; Carbs: 30g;
Fiber: 3g; Protein: 3g; Sodium: 308mg

TO MAKE THE RELISH

In a medium bowl, stir together the corn, pimentos, bell pepper, onion, and celery. Set aside.

TO MAKE THE DRESSING

1. In a small saucepan over medium heat, combine the sugar, vegetable oil, vinegar, salt, and pepper. Bring to a boil, stirring constantly. Remove from the heat. Pour the dressing over the corn relish. Stir to coat. Garnish to taste with cilantro (if using).

2. Enjoy this side dish warm or chilled. It's really good at summer cookouts!

DID YOU KNOW?: Ears of corn always have an even number of rows, usually 16 rows per ear.

INGREDIENT TIP: If fresh corn is in season, boil 4 or 5 ears, cut the kernels from the cob, and use the cooked fresh kernels instead of a can of whole-kernel corn.

"THE TRUE SOUTHERN WATERMELON IS A BOON APART, AND NOT TO BE MENTIONED WITH COMMONER THINGS. IT IS CHIEF OF THIS WORLD'S LUXURIES, KING BY GRACE OF GOD OVER ALL THE FRUITS OF THE EARTH. WHEN ONE HAS TASTED IT, HE KNOWS WHAT THE ANGELS EAT. IT WAS NOT A SOUTHERN WATERMELON THAT EVE TOOK: WE KNOW IT BECAUSE SHE REPENTED."

—MARK TWAIN

WATERMELON SALSA

DF | GF | NF | V

New Favorite | MAKES ABOUT **4** CUPS

Once, my friend and I bought a yellow watermelon from a roadside farm stand somewhere in Georgia. We hadn't planned on buying anything that day, *much less a watermelon*, but the tiny stand selling produce on the side of some back road we'd wandered down looked too inviting to pass up. We realized our conundrum when we got back to the car and wanted to dig in. We could've waited until we got home, but we were hungry and young. After several unsuccessful attempts to open it with our bare hands and a plastic gas station knife, we decided to throw it on the pavement. It worked, and soon we had our bellies full of homegrown watermelon. When I discovered salsa could be made from fruit, I immediately went for my favorite—watermelon. One bite has me grinning like a possum. *For this recipe, though, I recommend using a knife to open the watermelon.*

¼ cup fresh cilantro leaves, chopped

¼ cup chopped jalapeño peppers

2 tablespoons white vinegar

1½ teaspoons minced garlic

2 teaspoons to 1 tablespoon sugar

½ teaspoon salt

2 cups finely chopped watermelon

1 medium yellow onion, diced

2 navel oranges, peeled and chopped

1. In a medium bowl, stir together the cilantro, jalapeños, vinegar, garlic, sugar, and salt.

2. Add the watermelon, onion, and orange. Stir, making sure the watermelon mixture is well coated. Cover and chill for 1 hour before serving.

HOW-TO TIP: To choose a ripe watermelon, look for one that feels heavy and sounds hollow when you thump it on the bottom.

PREP TIME: 20 minutes, plus 1 hour chilling time

PER SERVING (½ CUP): Calories: 47; Total fat: 0g; Saturated fat: 0g; Cholesterol: 0mg; Carbs: 12g; Fiber: 2g; Protein: 1g; Sodium: 203mg

AMBROSIA

DF | **GF** | **V** | *Heirloom Recipe* | SERVES **4** TO **6**

Every Christmas, if I dared complain that Santa didn't bring me everything on my list, Mom would tell me I should be thankful for what I received. She'd end the story by telling me of her childhood Christmases, when the kids were each given an orange, a penny, and a handful of nuts from Santa. This could have been because she was one of 12 children. *And also probably explains why I am an only child.* Then she'd tell me the story, as she made this dish, of how their family always had a dish of ambrosia on Christmas Day and how much she enjoyed it. I wanted to ask if the kids had to contribute their nuts and oranges to make the ambrosia, but I was afraid she'd be offended. I'll never know the answer, but I do know we still have ambrosia during the holidays in memory of my mom.

8 large navel oranges, peeled
    and diced
1 cup shredded coconut
½ cup chopped pecans
½ cup maraschino cherries
1 (8-ounce) can crushed
    pineapple, drained
½ cup sugar

PREP TIME: 15 minutes

PER SERVING: Calories: 472; Total fat: 12g; Saturated fat: 8g; Cholesterol: 0mg; Carbs: 95g; Fiber: 12g; Protein: 5g; Sodium: 67mg

1. In a large bowl, stir together the oranges, coconut, pecans, cherries, and crushed pineapple.

2. Add the sugar and stir until blended. Cover and refrigerate until ready to serve.

DID YOU KNOW?: The word *ambrosia* comes from a Greek word meaning "immortal." In Greek mythology, only the gods could eat ambrosia.

INGREDIENT TIP: When we make this recipe in the summertime, we substitute fresh sliced peaches and strawberries for the oranges.

IN THE KITCHEN WITH CRISTAL WHITLOCK

Cristal, my friend and fellow church member, is an accomplished cook, always bringing a delicious dish to any meal. I asked her to share an easy dessert that's good for any church potluck, and this was her contribution.

—*Pam*

Anne's Easy Fudge

This fudge is named for Anne Patterson, whom I [Cristal] worked with back in the day. She was a little bit crazy but always the life of the party. To Anne's amusement (actually she thought I was crazy), I accidentally cooked this fudge *a bit* over 5 minutes and thought my house was about to burn down!

4 tablespoons (½ stick) salted butter, plus more for preparing the baking dish

2 cups sugar

⅓ cup corn syrup

½ cup whole milk

2 tablespoons cocoa powder

⅛ teaspoon salt

1 teaspoon vanilla extract

1 cup chopped walnuts or pecans (optional)

1. Grease a 9-by-9-inch baking dish with butter. Set aside.

2. In a medium saucepan, stir together the sugar, corn syrup, milk, cocoa powder, and salt. Place the pan over medium heat and bring the mixture to a boil. Boil for *exactly* 5 minutes.

3. Remove from the heat and stir in the vanilla and butter, stirring until the butter melts.

4. Using a handheld electric mixer, beat the fudge until it is glossy and thick.

5. Stir in the nuts (if using). Pour the fudge into the prepared baking dish. Let it harden, then cut it into squares.

PER SERVING (2 [1-INCH] SQUARES): Calories: 58; Total fat: 1g; Saturated fat: 1g; Cholesterol: 3mg; Carbs: 12g; Fiber: 0g; Protein: 0g; Sodium: 68mg

SAUSAGE BALLS IN CHEESE PASTRY

NF | *New Favorite* | MAKES **45** BALLS

My parents used to host a yearly Sunday school Christmas party. It was a lot of fun. Although it was for their Sunday school class, not mine, my best friend and I would hang around and help ourselves to the food. Every year, my mom's friend would say, "Tell Brittany I'm making sausage balls!" and every year I would excitedly wait for her arrival. I always offered to take the sausage balls to the table, popping a few in my mouth on the way. While waiting for the rest of the guests to arrive, I would surreptitiously snack on a few more. Honestly, it's a wonder any survived for the actual party! When Mom asked me what kind of recipes to put in this cookbook, my immediate response was "sausage balls." So here they are—but not your average, everyday sausage ball. When we discovered they could be made with a crust, we jumped on it.

FOR THE FILLING

1 pound pork sausage

¾ cup dry bread crumbs

⅓ cup chicken broth

3 tablespoons canola oil

FOR THE PASTRY

⅓ cup all-purpose flour

1 teaspoon paprika

¼ teaspoon salt

8 ounces grated sharp Cheddar cheese

8 tablespoons (1 stick) salted butter

PREP TIME: 20 minutes, plus 30 minutes chilling time

COOK TIME: 1 hour

PER SERVING (2 SAUSAGE BALLS):
Calories: 165; Total fat: 14g; Saturated fat: 6g; Cholesterol: 34mg; Carbs: 4g; Fiber: 0g; Protein: 6g; Sodium: 265mg

TO MAKE THE FILLING

1. In a medium bowl, mix together the sausage, bread crumbs, and chicken broth. Form the mixture into about 45 small balls.

2. In a skillet over medium-high heat, heat the canola oil.

3. Working in batches, place the sausage balls in the skillet. Fry for 4 to 5 minutes. Turn the balls and cook for 4 minutes more. Transfer to paper towel–lined plates to drain, and set them aside while you fry the remaining batches.

TO MAKE THE PASTRY

1. Sift the flour into a large bowl. Stir in the paprika and salt.

2. Add the Cheddar cheese and stir to combine.

3. Add the butter. Using a fork or pastry cutter, cut the butter into the flour and cheese mixture until blended. Spread the mixture onto a piece of wax paper.

4. Knead the dough for 3 to 5 minutes, until it is smooth, not sticky, more like a biscuit dough.

5. Pinch the dough into about 45 balls, using about 1 tablespoon of dough per ball.

TO ASSEMBLE THE SAUSAGE BALLS

1. Flatten a ball of dough and place a sausage ball in the center. Wrap the pastry around the sausage ball and pinch it closed. Repeat with the remaining pastry and sausage balls.

2. Place the assembled sausage balls in the freezer for 30 minutes.

3. Preheat the oven to 375°F.

4. Place the partially frozen balls on a baking sheet. Bake for 15 to 20 minutes or until the pastry is browned.

DID YOU KNOW?: Sausage was consumed in the civilization of ancient Sumer (where modern-day Iraq is located) more than 2,700 years ago!

DAIRY-FREE OPTION: Use vegan cheese in place of the Cheddar, and use vegan butter (we like Earth Balance Soy Free Buttery Spread).

GLUTEN-FREE OPTION: Use gluten-free all-purpose flour.

"THE SOUTH—THE PLACE WHERE MACARONI AND CHEESE IS A VEGETABLE."

—SOUTHERN SAYING

Four

—

SIDES AND SALADS

BRITTANY When I say I love salad, I get a lot of funny looks. Now, don't get me wrong, I do love a good green salad. *But around here, salad has a loose definition.* Salad is just a mixture of different ingredients with some kind of dressing or sauce to tie it together. Case in point: macaroni salad, pasta salad, congealed salad, and potato salad. None of those are the iceberg lettuce and sad, store-bought dressing salad most people think of! I also love side dishes. I can make a whole meal of the "and three" part of a meat and three, and I love tucking into a vegetable plate—of course, around here, macaroni and cheese counts as a vegetable. The key here is offering a nice, fresh-from-the-garden green salad alongside a heavier one. You feel indulgent, but you don't leave the table feeling like a little pleasure piggy. Luckily for you, we've done the heavy lifting when it comes to making some classic sides a little healthier. All you have to do is cook and enjoy.

WILTED LETTUCE SALAD

GF

Updated Classic | SERVES **4**

Bryan's dad, Bill, was an avid gardener. Each spring, before anything else could be planted, he would set out green onions and several types of lettuce. As soon as the lettuce and onions were ripe, Bryan's mom, Mary Frances, would make wilted lettuce salad. When Bryan and I were newly married, I tried to visit my in-laws near dinnertime so I could have salad, too. I visited so often that Mary Frances gave me the recipe and Bill began supplying me with lettuce and onions. Over the years, I began to make a fancier version, adding eggs, bacon, blue cheese, and pecans. This recipe is just as good today as it was when I first tried it.

FOR THE SALAD

1 large head buttercrunch lettuce, washed and dried

4 hard-boiled eggs, peeled and sliced

4 bacon slices, cooked and crumbled

½ cup chopped (½-inch pieces) scallions

¼ cup crumbled blue cheese

¼ cup pecans, toasted (see how-to tip on page 85)

FOR THE DRESSING

¼ cup vinegar of choice

¼ cup water

¼ cup sugar

2 tablespoons olive oil

PREP TIME: 30 minutes

PER SERVING: Calories: 328; Total fat: 23g; Saturated fat: 7g; Cholesterol: 191mg; Carbs: 16g; Fiber: 1g; Protein: 15g; Sodium: 623mg

NUT-FREE OPTION: Omit the pecans.

TO MAKE THE SALAD

1. Divide the lettuce among four salad bowls.

2. Top each salad with one-fourth of the sliced egg, one-fourth of the bacon, and 2 tablespoons of scallions.

TO MAKE THE DRESSING

1. In a small saucepan over medium-high heat, combine the vinegar, water, sugar, and olive oil. Cook, whisking, until the sugar dissolves. Pour the warm dressing over the salads.

2. Top each salad with 1 tablespoon of crumbled blue cheese and 1 tablespoon of toasted pecans. Serve immediately.

INGREDIENT TIP: Don't have buttercrunch lettuce? Substitute your favorite lettuce, Swiss chard, or spinach.

DAIRY-FREE OPTION: Omit the blue cheese.

PICKLED CUCUMBERS AND ONIONS

DF | GF | NF | V

Heirloom Recipe | SERVES **4**

I had a love/hate relationship with summer as a child. I loved the freedom of going barefoot, playing in the creek behind my grandmother's house, and eating fresh veggies straight from the vine. But the work involved in getting those fresh veggies? No thanks! To avoid gardening, I found a tree in the woods and spent a lot of time hiding, a book clutched in one hand. Once discovered, my grandmother would tell my mom, "Aw, Ina, leave her alone. She don't have to work. She'll have plenty of time for that when she's older." *There was a definite advantage to being the youngest grandchild.*

When my cousin and I spent the summer at my grandmother's, I offered a trade. She'd do the outdoor chores—including gardening—and I would cook. We both thought we had the better deal. This was one of the first recipes I learned to make, taught to me by Aunt Clois. If I want a different flavor, I sometimes substitute summer squash for the cucumbers.

3 cups white vinegar

½ cup sugar

1 teaspoon salt

1 teaspoon freshly ground
    black pepper

2 large cucumbers, trimmed, peeled,
    and cut into ½-inch-thick slices

1 large yellow onion, cut into
    ¼-inch-thick rings

1. In a small bowl, whisk the vinegar, sugar, salt, and pepper until blended.

2. Place the cucumbers and onions in a large bowl. Pour the vinegar mixture over them and stir until coated. Cover the bowl and refrigerate for at least 1 hour to chill. Stir before serving.

DID YOU KNOW?: Onions are one of the oldest cultivated vegetables. In the Middle Ages, onions were hung on door-frames to ward off the plague.

The phrase "cool as a cucumber" was first used by John Gay in 1732 in a poem entitled "A New Song of New Similes."

PREP TIME: 15 minutes, plus 1 hour chilling time

PER SERVING: Calories: 170; Total fat: 0g; Saturated fat: 0g; Cholesterol: 0mg; Carbs: 36g; Fiber: 2g; Protein: 2g; Sodium: 595mg

FREEZER SLAW

DF | **GF** | **NF** | **V**   *Heirloom Recipe* | SERVES **6** TO **8**

One of the first things Goonmomma taught me to make was slaw. She helped me grate the cabbage and carrots, toss it with the dressing, and season it with salt and pepper. We put it in the fridge and waited for Goondaddy to get home from wherever he was. We were going on a picnic, and we had all the classics: freezer slaw, macaroni salad, and potato salad. We also had baloney sandwiches, because that's what Goondaddy liked. I liked slaw. I liked making it, I liked eating it, and I liked making my family eat it after I made it. "The good thing about slaw," Goonmomma said as we waited, "is you can add whatever you want." "I'm going to add cucumbers," I said. "Except cucumbers," she said. I'm still slightly upset about those cucumbers, but I do enjoy this slaw.

FOR THE SLAW

1 small (about 2-pound) head
    green cabbage, shredded
1 medium green bell pepper, diced
1 medium red bell pepper, diced
1 medium yellow onion, diced
1 cup sugar

FOR THE DRESSING

6 tablespoons white vinegar
½ cup vegetable oil
1 teaspoon salt
1 teaspoon celery seed

PREP TIME: 15 minutes, plus 4 hours chilling time

COOK TIME: 10 minutes

PER SERVING: Calories: 337; Total fat: 19g; Saturated fat: 4g; Cholesterol: 0mg; Carbs: 45g; Fiber: 4g; Protein: 2g; Sodium: 412mg

TO MAKE THE SLAW

In a large bowl, combine the cabbage, green and red bell peppers, onion, and sugar. Stir to combine. Cover the bowl and refrigerate for 2 hours.

TO MAKE THE DRESSING

1. In a saucepan over medium heat, combine the vinegar, vegetable oil, salt, and celery seed. Bring to a boil, stirring constantly until the salt dissolves. Pour the dressing over the chilled cabbage mixture. Stir to coat the vegetables in the dressing.

2. Cover the bowl and chill for 2 hours before serving.

MAKE-AHEAD TIP: This slaw will keep for several days in the refrigerator, or it can be frozen in airtight plastic freezer containers. We used to make many containers of this in summer and store it in the freezer. *That's where it got its name.* Thaw in the refrigerator before serving.

VARIATION TIP: To turn this into a crunchy, Asian-inspired slaw, add one package of ramen noodles, without the flavor packet, and ½ cup sliced toasted pecans.

CORN BREAD SALAD

NF | **V**

Updated Classic | SERVES **8**

When I was a child, *I did not like corn bread.* I know. What Southerner does not like corn bread? As I grew older, I discovered I did like corn bread—just not my mom's. She liked crust. Since she was the cook, it was her way or the highway. She made her corn bread about a half inch thick, so it was mostly crust. Yuck! I liked the mound of tasty goodness between the crusts.

Everyone has their opinion on corn bread, and it's a hot debate. Sweet or not? Crusty or not? Added fillings? But one thing I've never heard anyone disagree about: Corn bread salad is delicious. I first tried this at a church dinner when I was a teen, and I was hooked. The pastor's wife, Flossie, shared the recipe, and I've been making it ever since—sometimes with a flavor twist like Cheddar cheese, or with turkey bacon to make it a little healthier. This recipe, though, was always an easy way to get my kids to eat some veggies.

FOR THE SALAD

2½ cups (about ¾ of a loaf) corn bread (see Broccoli Corn Bread variation tip, page 13)

1 medium green bell pepper, diced

1 medium yellow onion, diced

3 medium tomatoes, peeled and diced

½ cup bread-and-butter pickles, chopped

12 bacon slices, cooked and crumbled

FOR THE DRESSING

1 cup mayonnaise

1 tablespoon sugar

¼ cup bread-and-butter pickle juice

½ teaspoon salt

½ teaspoon freshly ground black pepper

PREP TIME: 30 minutes, plus 2 hours chilling time

PER SERVING: Calories: 353; Total fat: 23g; Saturated fat: 5g; Cholesterol: 39mg; Carbs: 23g; Fiber: 1g; Protein: 13g; Sodium: 1200mg

TO MAKE THE SALAD

1. Crumble the corn bread into medium pieces and transfer them to a large bowl or trifle dish.

2. Spread the bell pepper over the corn bread.

3. Spread the onion on top of the bell pepper.

4. Spread the tomatoes on top of the onion.

5. Top the tomatoes with the chopped pickles.

6. Top the pickles with the crumbled bacon.

TO MAKE THE DRESSING

In a small bowl, stir together the mayonnaise, sugar, pickle juice, salt, and pepper. Drizzle the dressing over the crumbled bacon. Cover the bowl tightly and refrigerate for 2 hours for the flavors to blend.

INGREDIENT TIP: If you're serving a crowd, simply double the recipe and layer into a trifle dish for a fancy presentation.

VARIATION TIP: Spice up this salad with Mexican corn bread. It's a recipe I've enjoyed since I was a kid—and it seems everyone in the South has their own version. Make the basic corn bread recipe (see Broccoli Corn Bread variation tip, page 13) and add 1 cup cream-style corn, 1 chopped medium green or red bell pepper, 1 cup grated Cheddar cheese, 1 diced small onion, and 1 chopped small jalapeño pepper. Preheat the oven to 375°F and bake for approximately 40 minutes or until a knife inserted into the center comes out clean.

VEGAN OPTION: Omit the bacon and use vegan mayonnaise and vegan sugar.

NEWFANGLED CREAMED CORN

| GF | NF | V |

New Favorite | SERVES **4**

Whenever we had corn for dinner, the kids never knew when I would feel the need to tell "The Corn Story." It was a grim warning about misbehaving and, naturally, my kids thought it was hilarious. "Once when I was 17," I began, "a friend and I drove to town to see and be seen. It was a warm fall evening, and we were sitting on the hood of my car, talking, when some friends drove up. We stepped over to talk to them, noticing a 24-pack of toilet paper in the back of their truck. 'We're bored,' they said. 'We're going to TP some yards.' 'Huh,' I said, 'I've never TPed a yard before.' 'Me either,' my friend chimed in. 'Come with us,' they said." We, being young and apparently having lost our senses, climbed into the truck. The evening quickly went downhill and ended with us driving into a cornfield by accident. We were never tempted to TP a yard again. Even without a corn story of your own, this dish (created for unexpected company!) will quickly become a favorite.

Nonstick cooking spray

2 (14.5-ounce) cans whole-kernel corn, drained, or fresh corn (see ingredient tip)

4 ounces cream cheese, at room temperature

1 (3-ounce) package garlic and herb goat cheese

¾ cup fresh bread crumbs (see how-to tip)

2 teaspoons Italian seasoning or herbes de Provence

1. Preheat the oven to 350°F. Coat a 2-quart casserole dish with cooking spray, and set it aside.

2. In a medium bowl, combine the corn, cream cheese, and goat cheese. Stir until blended.

3. In a small bowl, combine the bread crumbs and Italian seasoning.

4. Pour the corn mixture into the prepared casserole dish. Sprinkle the seasoned bread crumbs on top.

5. Cover the dish with aluminum foil and bake for 20 to 25 minutes or until the mixture is heated through and bubbly.

PREP TIME: 15 minutes

COOK TIME: 20 to 25 minutes

PER SERVING: Calories: 372; Total fat: 18g; Saturated fat: 10g; Cholesterol: 52mg; Carbs: 46g; Fiber: 5g; Protein: 13g; Sodium: 350mg

HOW-TO TIP: Make your own bread crumbs: Slice some bread (I use French bread) and put several slices in a food processor or blender. Process for 10 to 15 seconds. Get creative and add cheese or herbs to make seasoned bread crumbs. Parmesan cheese and Italian seasoning make a great combination.

INGREDIENT TIP: If fresh corn is in season, boil eight ears and cut the kernels off the cob. Use the cooked fresh kernels instead of the two cans of whole-kernel corn.

GLUTEN-FREE OPTION: Use gluten-free bread crumbs.

"TWO INGREDIENTS DEAR TO ANY SOUTHERNER'S HEART: HOGS AND CORN."

—"MISS ROBBIE" MONTGOMERY

FRIED GREEN TOMATOES WITH GARLIC AIOLI

NF | V   *Updated Classic* | SERVES **4**

When I was younger, my parents took us on a vacation to Warm Springs, Georgia. Although it was interesting to see the place where Franklin D. Roosevelt had soaked in the springs, hoping for relief from his polio, one of my most vivid memories is the food. We stopped at a restaurant in downtown Warm Springs and ate on the patio. I don't remember what entrées we ordered, but I'll always remember our appetizers. We had fried pickles and fried green tomatoes. They were crispy, crunchy, and I thought they were the best things I had ever eaten in my life. I was determined to re-create those fried green tomatoes at home! At the restaurant, they were served with homemade ranch dressing for dipping. I've grown up, and my taste buds have too, so now I serve them with garlic aioli.

FOR THE GARLIC AIOLI

¾ cup mayonnaise

2 tablespoons minced garlic

2½ teaspoons freshly squeezed
    lemon juice

½ to 1 teaspoon salt

½ teaspoon freshly ground
    black pepper

PREP TIME: 20 minutes, plus 30 minutes chilling time

COOK TIME: 4 to 6 minutes per batch

PER SERVING: Calories: 559; Total fat: 26g; Saturated fat: 5g; Cholesterol: 105mg; Carbs: 72g; Fiber: 5g; Protein: 12g; Sodium: 1591mg

FOR THE TOMATOES

2 large eggs

2 tablespoons whole or 2% milk

1 cup all-purpose flour

1 cup self-rising cornmeal

1 to 2 teaspoons salt

1 teaspoon freshly ground
    black pepper

3 medium green tomatoes, cut
    into slices ¼ to ½ inch thick
    (I prefer ¼ inch)

Vegetable oil, for frying

TO MAKE THE AIOLI

In a small bowl, stir together the mayonnaise, garlic, lemon juice, salt, and pepper until blended. Refrigerate for at least 30 minutes.

TO MAKE THE TOMATOES

1. In a shallow bowl, whisk the eggs and milk.

2. Put the flour in another shallow bowl.

3. In a third shallow bowl, stir together the cornmeal, salt, and pepper.

4. Dip the tomatoes first in the egg mixture and then in the flour.

5. Dip the tomatoes in the egg mixture again and then into the cornmeal.

6. In a skillet over medium-high heat, heat about ½ cup of vegetable oil.

7. Working in batches, place the tomato slices in the skillet, making sure they do not touch. Fry for 2 to 3 minutes, then flip the tomatoes and fry for 2 to 3 minutes more, or until brown.

8. Transfer the tomatoes to paper towel–lined plates to drain. Add more oil to the skillet between batches, as needed. Serve hot with the garlic aioli.

MAKE-AHEAD TIP: The aioli can be made up to 24 hours ahead and stored in an airtight container in the refrigerator.

DAIRY-FREE AND VEGAN OPTION: Substitute water for the milk, use melted vegan butter instead of the egg mixture, and use vegan mayonnaise.

GLUTEN-FREE OPTION: Use gluten-free all-purpose flour.

"IT'S DIFFICULT TO THINK ANYTHING BUT PLEASANT THOUGHTS WHILE EATING A HOMEGROWN TOMATO."

—LEWIS GRIZZARD

CHEESY SQUASH

GF | NF | V

New Favorite | SERVES **8**

Squash is abundant during summer. At the farmers' market where I work, you can get pounds of it for cheap. At the end of the day, *the farmers practically throw it at you* to get rid of it. I'm all about free food, so I spend a bit of each day sweet-talking my way into taking the squash off the hands of the people around us. As plain squash can be pretty bland, I then spend quite a bit of time coming up with creative ways to use it. Because I work at a cheese stand, I also take home some cheese every Sunday. Combining my cheese and my squash just made sense to me, and this cheesy squash recipe was born. Take advantage of summer's bounty and make this for yourself. Don't like Parmesan? Substitute your favorite cheese instead. Gouda and provolone make good substitutes.

Nonstick cooking spray

6 small zucchini or yellow squash (or a mix), cut into 1-inch-thick slices

¼ cup olive oil

1 teaspoon garlic powder

½ teaspoon salt (optional)

½ teaspoon freshly ground black pepper (optional)

½ cup grated Parmesan cheese

PREP TIME: 15 minutes

COOK TIME: 40 minutes

PER SERVING: Calories: 102; Total fat: 8g; Saturated fat: 2g; Cholesterol: 5mg; Carbs: 5g; Fiber: 2g; Protein: 4g; Sodium: 80mg

1. Preheat the oven to 400°F. Coat a 9-by-13-inch baking dish with cooking spray (or see variation tip).

2. Place the squash slices in the prepared baking dish and drizzle with the olive oil.

3. In a small bowl, combine the garlic powder with the salt and pepper (if using). Sprinkle it evenly over the squash, followed by the Parmesan.

4. Bake for 30 minutes or until golden brown.

VARIATION TIP: If it's too darn hot to turn on the oven, heat 3 tablespoons of olive oil in a skillet over medium-high heat. When hot, add the squash, spices, and Parmesan. Sauté for 5 to 10 minutes or until the squash is tender, stirring often.

DAIRY-FREE AND VEGAN OPTION: Use vegan cheese.

HERBED SKILLET POTATOES

GF | **NF** | **V** *New Favorite* | SERVES **4**

Potatoes are possibly the most versatile vegetable—mashed for an everyday dinner, fried to go with a burger, scalloped for brunch, or made into soup for a cold winter's night. Here, we've tried something a little different. I like to use fresh herbs from our garden during spring and summer for this dish. There's nothing better than using something you've grown, and it gives the dish a delightful, fresh flavor. We've toyed with the idea of growing our own potatoes—but then I remember helping Goondaddy pick sweet potatoes in his garden, *and I decide against it.* Store-bought potatoes will do me just fine until I can rope my husband into growing and picking the potatoes for me. He'll never know what hit him, but he may think it's worth it for this recipe.

2 tablespoons salted butter

1 medium green bell pepper, chopped

1 small yellow onion, diced

¼ cup grated Parmesan cheese

2 teaspoons chopped fresh basil or
     ½ teaspoon dried

2 teaspoons fresh rosemary leaves
     or ½ teaspoon dried

2 teaspoons fresh oregano leaves or
     ½ teaspoon dried

½ teaspoon seasoned salt

½ teaspoon freshly ground
     black pepper

¼ teaspoon garlic powder

3 large Irish potatoes, peeled and cut
     into ¼-inch slices

PREP TIME: 20 minutes

COOK TIME: 20 minutes

PER SERVING: Calories: 360; Total fat: 11g; Saturated fat: 7g; Cholesterol: 30mg; Carbs: 53g; Fiber: 8g; Protein: 12g; Sodium: 490mg

1. In a large skillet over medium heat, melt the butter.

2. Add the bell pepper, onion, Parmesan, basil, rosemary, oregano, salt, pepper, and garlic powder. Stir well to combine.

3. Add the potatoes and stir to coat. Cook for about 20 minutes, stirring frequently, until the potatoes are easily pierced with a fork.

DID YOU KNOW?: A baked potato with the skin on has more than twice the potassium of a banana.

VARIATION TIP: For a different flavor, try Havarti or Muenster instead of the Parmesan.

DAIRY-FREE AND VEGAN OPTION: Use vegan butter and vegan cheese.

EASY MARINATED HERBED CAULIFLOWER AND CHICKPEAS

DF | **GF** | **NF** | **V**

New Favorite | SERVES **6**

Until I went gluten free, I refused to eat cauliflower. I always thought of it as broccoli's boring cousin. After I went gluten free, cauliflower began to pop up in unusual places, like pizza crusts. When my daughter was diagnosed with a milk allergy, cauliflower showed up even more, in cheese substitutes and "Alfredo" sauces. Now, I've come to terms with cauliflower. I keep a head in my fridge at all times for buffalo cauliflower, dairy-free "cream" sauces, and recipes like this easy, veggie-forward herbed cauliflower. Marinated vegetables have always been one of my favorite picnic foods, and this crunchy cauliflower and chickpea dish is perfect as a side for all your summer cookouts. Even though it takes 4 hours to chill while the flavors combine, it's worth the wait. I promise.

⅓ cup olive oil

⅓ cup red wine vinegar

1 tablespoon chopped fresh parsley

1 tablespoon chopped fresh basil

1 teaspoon salt

¼ teaspoon freshly ground black pepper

1 large tomato, cut into ½-inch-thick slices

1 (15-ounce) can chickpeas, rinsed and drained

½ cauliflower head, chopped into 1-inch pieces

1 small yellow onion, diced

1. In a medium jar with a lid, combine the olive oil, vinegar, parsley, basil, salt, and pepper. Cover the jar and set it aside.

2. In a shallow bowl, combine the tomato, chickpeas, cauliflower, and onion.

3. Shake the dressing until combined. Pour it over the vegetables and toss them lightly with a fork until completely coated. Refrigerate for 4 hours to marinate.

MAKE-AHEAD TIP: This recipe can be made 24 hours in advance and refrigerated until ready to eat.

DID YOU KNOW?: In the 1700s, many Europeans were afraid of tomatoes. They were nicknamed the "poison apple" because the aristocracy believed eating them caused sickness or death.

PREP TIME: 15 minutes, plus 4 hours chilling time

PER SERVING: Calories: 217; Total fat: 12g; Saturated fat: 2g; Cholesterol: 0mg; Carbs: 23g; Fiber: 5g; Protein: 5g; Sodium: 644mg

CORN AND TOMATO SKILLET

| GF | NF | V |

New Favorite | SERVES **4** TO **6**

Our former next-door neighbor, a sweet elderly man named Mr. Smith, planted a garden each spring, including 10 tomato plants. He worked magic with those plants, the vines bending under the weight of tomatoes he shared with everyone on our street. Meanwhile, each year I struggled with my two scraggly tomato plants. I didn't worry, though, because Mr. Smith would appear on my doorstep with green tomatoes for frying or ripe tomatoes for salads. When he died, I took a sympathy card around the neighborhood for everyone to sign for his family. After commenting on what a nice man and wonderful neighbor he was, everyone wondered, "Now who will grow our tomatoes?" *This recipe is dedicated to you, Mr. Smith; I know you would have loved it.* This dish can be made a day in advance and kept refrigerated until ready to heat and serve.

1 to 2 teaspoons salted butter

1 (14.5-ounce) can whole-kernel corn, drained, or fresh corn (see ingredient tip)

1 (14.5-ounce) can creamed corn

3 medium tomatoes, peeled and chopped

½ cup sliced scallions

2 teaspoons Italian seasoning or herbes de Provence

PREP TIME: 10 minutes

COOK TIME: 20 minutes

PER SERVING: Calories: 176; Total fat: 3g; Saturated fat: 1g; Cholesterol: 4mg; Carbs: 38g; Fiber: 5g; Protein: 5g; Sodium: 318mg

In a medium skillet over medium-high heat, combine the butter, whole-kernel corn, creamed corn, tomatoes, scallions, and seasoning. Bring the mixture to a boil. Reduce the heat to low and simmer for 15 to 20 minutes.

HOW-TO TIP: Make your own Italian seasoning: Blend together 2 teaspoons of dried oregano, 2 teaspoons of dried basil, 2 teaspoons of dried marjoram, and 1 teaspoon of dried sage. Store in an airtight container.

INGREDIENT TIP: If fresh corn is in season, boil four ears of corn and cut the kernels off the cob. Use the cooked fresh kernels instead of one can of whole-kernel corn.

DAIRY-FREE AND VEGAN OPTION: Use vegan butter.

VEGETABLE BEEF SOUP WITH NOODLES *page 72*

Five

THAT REALLY STIRS MY STEW

—

SOUPS, STEW, AND CHILI

PAM There's nothing like a steaming hot bowl of soup on a winter evening. *Or, since I am cold natured, below 65 degrees Fahrenheit.* My favorite soup memory involves a blizzard. Now, a blizzard might not seem unusual in many parts of the country, but in Georgia, a huge snowstorm is two or three inches. This was the first blizzard in our area in more than 100 years. As soon as the storm hit, the electricity went out and stayed off for the next 48 hours. As the temperature in our home dropped to 38 degrees, we took our three-month-old and trudged next door to Bryan's grandmother's house. She had a huge gas heater that kept one room at a balmy 90 degrees while the other rooms stayed a chilly 40. We spent our time either sweating or freezing. We used her antique wood stove, located in a cutesy sitting room added on to my father-in-law's workshop, to prepare soup for dinner. I felt transported back to the '30s, with the portable radio as the only entertainment. Grandmother hid a candy bar in her chair and, whenever she thought we weren't looking, would sneak a bite. I hope our soup recipes help you create loving memories you can enjoy, even without the blizzard.

TOMATO BASIL SOUP

GF | **NF** | **V** *New Favorite* | SERVES **8** TO **10**

Weird fact: I have a deviated septum. Between my crooked nose and my seasonal allergies, I spend most of the spring and fall with a stuffed-up face. I'm not alone in my suffering, though, and that's probably why everyone around here likes soup so much. Nothing makes you feel better when you're sick than a steaming bowl of hot soup. Although much of the world prefers some variety of chicken noodle, at my house, it's all about the tomato. As soon as I hear someone sniffle, I'm in the kitchen, whipping up a big batch of this soup. By the time you can say, "Bless you," I already have the can of tomatoes open and in the pot. I like to serve this soup with a pimento grilled cheese on the side. Its secret, though, is the fresh basil (but see variation tip).

8 tablespoons (1 stick) salted butter, divided
1 medium yellow onion, chopped
1 celery stalk, chopped
2 tablespoons minced garlic
2 (28-ounce) cans tomatoes, undrained
1 carrot, thinly sliced
¾ cup heavy (whipping) cream
¾ cup whole milk
¼ cup chopped fresh basil
1 to 2 teaspoons salt
½ teaspoon freshly ground black pepper

PREP TIME: 30 minutes

COOK TIME: 1 hour, 30 minutes

PER SERVING: Calories: 229; Total fat: 20g; Saturated fat: 12g; Cholesterol: 58mg; Carbs: 12g; Fiber: 3g; Protein: 4g; Sodium: 407mg

1. In a stockpot over medium heat, melt 4 tablespoons (½ stick) of butter.

2. Stir in the onion and celery. Cook for about 2 minutes, until transparent.

3. Add the garlic. Cook for 30 seconds.

4. Add the tomatoes and carrot. Bring the mixture to a boil.

5. Reduce the heat to low and simmer for 1 hour.

6. Let the soup cool slightly. After cooling, transfer the soup to a blender and process it to a sauce-like consistency, working in batches if needed. Return the soup to the pot and place the pot back over low heat.

7. Add the remaining 4 tablespoons of butter, the cream, milk, basil, salt, and pepper. Stir until blended and heated through.

INGREDIENT TIP: If you prefer, use 2% milk instead of whole milk, but the soup will be thinner.

MAKE-AHEAD TIP: If you would like to freeze the soup, stop after blending the soup (step 6) and freeze it in an airtight container. When ready to use, thaw the soup in the refrigerator, heat it over low heat until warm, and continue with the recipe as written.

VARIATION TIP: Don't like basil? Substitute ¼ cup fresh oregano or fresh rosemary instead.

DAIRY-FREE AND VEGAN OPTION: Use vegan whipping cream or soft tofu, soy milk, and vegan butter.

CREAM OF BROCCOLI AND CAULIFLOWER SOUP

NF | V

New Favorite | SERVES **6** TO **8**

One of my favorite places to go is a local tearoom. They have everything I love: fancy hats, Earl Grey, cutesy decor, beautiful teacups, and cream of broccoli soup. I love nothing better than getting dolled up and having afternoon tea there. Sometimes, though, I don't feel like going to all the effort of putting on makeup and curling my hair. On those days, I'm grateful that my mom's neighbor gave us this delicious recipe for cream of broccoli soup. Now that I've come to love cauliflower, I add this veggie to give it a twist, but you could double the broccoli in this recipe if you prefer to keep it traditional. I like to keep the ingredients for this soup on hand because I never know when a craving will strike.

3 tablespoons salted butter

1 small yellow onion, diced

3 tablespoons all-purpose flour

3 cups whole milk

1 cup vegetable broth or chicken broth

¾ cup chopped cooked broccoli

¾ cup chopped cooked cauliflower

2 teaspoons salt

½ teaspoon freshly ground black pepper

PREP TIME: 15 minutes

COOK TIME: 25 minutes

PER SERVING: Calories: 157; Total fat: 10g; Saturated fat: 6g; Cholesterol: 10mg; Carbs: 11g; Fiber: 1g; Protein: 6g; Sodium: 1000mg

1. In a stockpot over medium heat, melt the butter.

2. Add the onion. Cook for about 5 minutes, until tender.

3. Stir in the flour.

4. Slowly add the milk, stirring constantly.

5. Stir in the vegetable broth. Cook the soup for 10 to 15 minutes, until smooth and thick, stirring frequently.

6. Add the broccoli, cauliflower, salt, and pepper. Simmer for 5 more minutes, until heated through.

INGREDIENT TIP: Cooked asparagus can be substituted for the broccoli.

DAIRY-FREE AND VEGAN OPTION: Use vegan butter and soy milk instead of the dairy products.

GLUTEN-FREE OPTION: Use gluten-free all-purpose flour.

GRANDMOTHER'S POTATO SOUP

GF | NF | V   *Heirloom Recipe* | SERVES **4**

One semester, my junior year of college, and a few months after I got married, I had to work 40 hours in a local elementary school for one of my classes. Of course, this was when cold and flu season hit and everyone was sick. I spent most of the semester recovering from one illness so I could catch another. Strep throat, the flu, a stomach virus—you name it, I had it. One day, when I was lying on my bed wishing I didn't have classes or homework, I heard a knock on my door. It was Bryan's Grandmother Reeves, who knew I was sick and had brought me a bowl of potato soup. Although I was sure I didn't like potato soup, I thanked her. I ate it because I was hungry and too tired to fix something myself. I was surprised by how good it was. Grandmother gave me the recipe and I serve it even when we aren't sick.

3 medium Irish potatoes, peeled and shredded
½ teaspoon salt
1 (5-ounce) can evaporated milk
2 tablespoons salted butter
1 teaspoon freshly ground black pepper

PREP TIME: 15 minutes

COOK TIME: 20 minutes

PER SERVING: Calories: 210; Total fat: 9g; Saturated fat: 5g; Cholesterol: 3mg; Carbs: 29g; Fiber: 4g; Protein: 5g; Sodium: 376mg

VARIATION TIP: Want to give this a slightly different taste? Substitute 2 cups cooked and mashed cauliflower for the potatoes.

DAIRY-FREE AND VEGAN OPTION: Use 5 ounces of soy milk and vegan butter in place of the dairy products.

1. Place the potatoes in a stockpot and add enough water to just cover them.

2. Add the salt and place the pot over high heat. Bring to a boil. Reduce the heat to medium and cook for 15 minutes or until the potatoes are soft, stirring occasionally.

3. Add the evaporated milk, butter, and pepper to the soup. Heat until the butter melts, stirring occasionally.

DID YOU KNOW?: In older recipes, you might see ingredients such as "butter the size of a hen's egg." If you do, no need to worry. That's been calculated to equal 2 tablespoons.

HOW-TO TIP: To store potatoes, keep them in a cool, well-ventilated area—but not in the refrigerator, as this causes discoloration and a change in flavor.

CHEESE SOUP

Updated Classic | SERVES **4**

One year, Mom put Ashton and me in charge of planning our Christmas Eve menu. Our fancy Christmas meal is lunch on Christmas Day, where we join extended family for a big meal and presents. On Christmas Eve, it's just our immediate family. This means it's a casual meal, usually something simple like soup and sandwiches. We decided on grilled cheese sandwiches, queso dip, and this cheese soup. It was a lot of cheese, *and we're no longer allowed to design holiday menus*. However, this cheesy soup is still a favorite in our family. We've updated it a bit with turkey bacon, and we're big fans of black beans instead of kidney beans.

4 turkey bacon or bacon slices

1 medium yellow onion, chopped

1 medium green bell pepper, chopped

1 (14.5-ounce) can black beans or
    kidney beans, rinsed and drained

3 medium tomatoes, peeled
    and chopped

1 teaspoon chili powder

1 teaspoon salt

½ teaspoon freshly ground
    black pepper

¾ cup shredded sharp Cheddar
    cheese or Monterey Jack cheese

PREP TIME: 15 minutes

COOK TIME: 25 minutes

PER SERVING: Calories: 271; Total fat: 15g; Saturated fat: 7g; Cholesterol: 40mg; Carbs: 17g; Fiber: 5g; Protein: 17g; Sodium: 1729mg

1. In a stockpot over medium heat, cook the bacon until crisp. Transfer the bacon to a paper towel–lined plate, leaving the drippings in the pot.

2. Add the onion and bell pepper to the bacon drippings. Sauté for 2 to 3 minutes, until tender.

3. Stir in the black beans, tomatoes, chili powder, salt, and pepper. Simmer for 5 to 10 minutes.

4. Crumble the bacon and add it to the pot along with the cheese. Stir to combine. Simmer for about 5 minutes more, until the cheese is melted.

HOW-TO TIP: Before grating your cheese, apply a thin coat of vegetable oil to both sides of the grater. The cheese will slide right off!

INGREDIENT TIP: Use one (14.5-ounce) can of diced tomatoes instead of fresh tomatoes.

CABBAGE BEEF SOUP

DF | GF | NF

Updated Classic | SERVES **6**

The weather in the South is weird. Sometimes, especially in spring and fall, you can have all four seasons in one week. *Seriously*. One day it's 77 degrees. The next day it's 38 and I am forced to rush outside to cover my plants. I am one of those people who likes to plant herbs, veggies, and flowers at the first sign of spring, ignoring the warnings about waiting until the optimal planting time in our area. I always lose one or two plants, thanks to my impatience. The one good thing about our early spring and late fall weather is it is the perfect temperature for growing cabbage. That makes it easy to pick a fresh head whenever the temperature drops to 38 degrees and I need a bowl of soup to warm me up. This soup gets an updated kick from the chili powder. If you don't have any, substitute an equal amount of taco seasoning.

1½ pounds ground beef
1 medium yellow onion, diced
1 medium green bell pepper, diced
1 small (about 1-pound) head cabbage, shredded
1 (28-ounce) can diced tomatoes
1 teaspoon chili powder or taco seasoning
1 (16-ounce) can kidney beans, rinsed and drained
1 teaspoon salt

PREP TIME: 20 minutes

COOK TIME: 50 minutes

PER SERVING: Calories: 298; Total fat: 9g; Saturated fat: 3g; Cholesterol: 70mg; Carbs: 28g; Fiber: 10g; Protein: 29g; Sodium: 726mg

INGREDIENT TIP: If a recipe says, "Boil cabbage until tender," place shredded cabbage in boiling water for 5 minutes and it will be perfectly tender.

1. In a skillet over medium heat, cook the ground beef for about 10 minutes, breaking it up with a spoon, or until browned. Drain the meat and transfer it to a stockpot.

2. Add the onion and bell pepper. Cover the mixture with enough water to barely cover the meat (about 2 cups). Turn the heat to high and cook for 10 minutes.

3. Stir in the cabbage, tomatoes, chili powder, kidney beans, and salt. Bring the soup to a boil. Reduce the heat to medium-low, cover the pot, and simmer for 30 minutes, stirring occasionally.

DID YOU KNOW?: Onions were considered symbols of eternity in ancient Egypt. When Pharaoh Ramses IV's body was discovered, scientists found traces of onion in his eye sockets.

SMOKY CHEESY BEAN SOUP

GF | NF

New Favorite | SERVES **8**

Bean soup is a long time favorite in my family. It's filling and low-cost, plus many of my bean soup recipes can be prepared in a slow cooker. Coming home from work in the evening and having dinner ready, except for throwing a loaf of French bread or corn bread into the oven, is heavenly.

When I was pregnant with my daughter, I turned green whenever I smelled food. To be sure Bryan still had dinner, I would hastily prepare a batch of this soup, place it in the slow cooker, and take it to the cutesy sitting room located outside of my father-in-law's workshop. I would rush in occasionally to check on the soup, holding my breath to avoid any cooking odors. Bryan would have a home-cooked meal (a rarity during that pregnancy), and I avoided turning green. We simplified our recipe to use only white beans, but you can use one pound of your favorite mixed beans, if you prefer. Now, I'm happy to prepare this soup and enjoy the aroma.

1 pound dried white beans

1 cup diced cooked ham

2 bay leaves

1 teaspoon salt

1 teaspoon freshly ground black pepper

3 large Irish potatoes, diced

3 carrots, cut into 1-inch pieces

1 large yellow onion, chopped

2 or 3 drops liquid smoke (optional)

1 cup shredded Parmesan cheese

PREP TIME: 20 minutes, plus overnight soaking

COOK TIME: 2 to 3 hours

PER SERVING: Calories: 371; Total fat: 5g; Saturated fat: 2g; Cholesterol: 17mg; Carbs: 61g; Fiber: 13g; Protein: 23g; Sodium: 714mg

1. Rinse the beans in a colander and sort through them for any debris. Put the beans in a large bowl and add cold water (you'll need 4 cups of water for each cup of beans) to cover. Cover the bowl tightly, and set it aside to soak for at least 8 hours or overnight. Drain the beans and transfer them to a stockpot.

2. Add enough fresh water to cover the beans by 2 inches.

3. Add the ham, bay leaves, salt, and pepper to the pot. Turn the heat to high and bring the mixture to a boil. Reduce the heat to medium and simmer the soup until the beans are tender. Begin checking the beans after 1 hour, as the cooking time will vary depending on the size and age of the beans.

4. Add the potatoes, carrots, onion, and liquid smoke (if using) to the soup. Simmer for 30 minutes or until the vegetables are soft.

5. Remove the pot from the heat and stir in the cheese. Remove and discard the bay leaves before serving.

HOW-TO TIP: To cook this soup more quickly, cut all the ingredients into small pieces that are roughly the same size.

CHICKEN NOODLE SOUP

DF | NF

Heirloom Recipe | SERVES **8**

My mother believed chicken noodle soup cured everything—from the common cold to a greasy scalp. *Okay, maybe not the greasy scalp.* She made it whenever I was sick. As I had allergies that turned into a sinus infection whenever the weather changed, I ate chicken noodle soup often. I preferred my chicken noodle soup with lots of noodles and shredded chicken. Since my mom died 16 years ago, I'd forgotten how nice it was to have a bowl of steaming chicken noodle soup delivered to me when I was under the weather. Recently I had surgery, and my sweet neighbor Mary brought me a steaming pot full of chicken noodle soup. I was instantly transported back to my childhood. You don't have to be sick to enjoy this soup; it's delicious anytime.

2 or 3 boneless, skinless chicken breasts

3 quarts water

2 carrots, cut into 1-inch pieces

2 medium Irish potatoes, diced

1 medium yellow onion, diced

1 celery stalk, cut into ½-inch pieces

3 chicken bouillon cubes

2 tablespoons chopped fresh parsley or ½ teaspoon dried

½ teaspoon onion powder

½ teaspoon garlic powder

½ teaspoon salt

½ teaspoon freshly ground black pepper

¼ teaspoon paprika

¼ teaspoon red pepper flakes

1 (12-ounce) package egg noodles, or any noodle you prefer

PREP TIME: 20 minutes

COOK TIME: 1 hour, plus 15 minutes standing time

PER SERVING: Calories: 147; Total fat: 2g; Saturated fat: 0g; Cholesterol: 29mg; Carbs: 24g; Fiber: 3g; Protein: 10g; Sodium: 345mg

1. In a stockpot over high heat, combine the chicken breasts and water. Bring chicken to a boil. Reduce the heat to medium-high. Cook for 20 minutes. Transfer the chicken to a plate to cool. Strain the chicken broth, return it to the pot, and place the pot back over the heat.

2. Add the carrots, potatoes, onion, and celery and bring to a boil. Reduce the heat to medium. Simmer for 15 minutes.

3. Stir in the chicken bouillon cubes, parsley, onion powder, garlic powder, salt, pepper, paprika, and red pepper flakes. Simmer for 5 to 10 minutes.

4. Stir in the noodles. Simmer for 5 minutes more or until the noodles are tender.

5. While the soup simmers, cut the chicken into 1-inch pieces.

6. Remove the pot from the heat and add the chicken pieces to the soup. Cover the pot and let stand for 15 minutes.

INGREDIENT TIP: If you're worried that you over-salted a soup or stew, add half of a medium Irish potato when cooking. Remove the potato before serving.

GLUTEN-FREE OPTION: Use gluten-free egg noodles.

VEGETABLE BEEF SOUP WITH NOODLES

DF | NF

New Favorite | SERVES **6**

In winter, it seemed there was always a pot of soup going on Grandmother's stove. No matter the occasion, the smell of soup welcomed you at the door. Being a proper Southern lady, Grandmother wouldn't let any of her family leave hungry. If you expressed the slightest interest in the soup, you'd be unceremoniously directed toward the table, where a bowl of soup and a piece of corn bread would be plopped down in front of you—always with a glass of tea and plenty of butter for the bread. If you finished one bowl, you'd be offered another. If you had declined the first bowl, you would be asked, "Are you sure? It's that vegetable soup you like," repeated until you either agreed to eat a bowl or left the house. It's good soup, so you should definitely eat a second bowl. As a proper Southern *modern* lady, when I serve this to my vegetarian and vegan friends, I use meat substitute and veggie broth. They ask for another bowl, too!

1 pound ground beef

1 garlic clove, crushed

10 cups water

2 beef bouillon cubes

1 (28-ounce) can diced tomatoes

½ small head cabbage, shredded

1 large yellow onion, diced

1 large yellow squash, sliced

1 large zucchini, sliced

1½ cups fresh okra, sliced

1 (14.5-ounce) can green beans, drained

1 (16-ounce) box macaroni noodles

PREP TIME: 30 minutes

COOK TIME: 35 minutes

PER SERVING: Calories: 475; Total fat: 7g; Saturated fat: 2g; Cholesterol: 47mg; Carbs: 75g; Fiber: 9g; Protein: 29g; Sodium: 297mg

1. In a medium skillet over medium heat, combine the ground beef and garlic. Cook for about 10 minutes, breaking up the beef with the back of a spoon, until browned. Drain the beef and transfer it to a soup pot.

2. Add the water and bouillon cubes. Turn the heat to high and bring the mixture to a boil. Reduce the heat to medium-high.

3. Add the tomatoes, cabbage, and onion to the soup pot, stirring to blend. Cook for 5 minutes.

4. Add the yellow squash and zucchini. Cook for about 5 minutes or until tender.

5. Add the okra, green beans, and the uncooked macaroni noodles. Cook for 10 more minutes, stirring often, until the macaroni is cooked through.

HOW-TO TIP: If you have leftover broth, you can fill ice-cube trays with beef broth and freeze. When the cubes are frozen, remove and keep frozen in plastic freezer bags. If using for this recipe, use 4 or 5 cubes, depending on taste.

GLUTEN-FREE OPTION: Substitute gluten-free macaroni.

VEGETARIAN OPTION: Substitute ½ cup of vegetable broth for the bouillon and leave out the meat.

OLD-FASHIONED BEEF STEW

DF | NF

Heirloom Recipe | SERVES **8**

Beef stew doesn't spring to mind when you think of Southern food, but, contrary to popular belief, we get winter here, too. For the full two days of it, we Georgians hunker down in our houses and refuse to leave, except to buy all the beef and milk and bread our grocery stores have on the shelves. You know, in case we see a snowflake. Why milk? Why bread? No one can answer those questions for me. *And trust me, I've asked.*

But why beef? Well, the threat of snow makes us Southerners crave a good, hearty soup. We crave tomato soup, vegetable soup, potato soup, and chili. A good, stick-to-your-ribs kind of meal that makes you forget it's a full 40 degrees outside. Most of all, we crave a hearty beef stew like this one, passed down for generations. To give this a punch of flavor, add 1 to 2 tablespoons of red wine when adding the water.

2 pounds beef stew meat, cut into
   1-inch pieces
½ cup all-purpose flour
4 teaspoons salt, divided
1 teaspoon freshly ground black pepper
2 tablespoons vegetable oil
6 cups water
2 beef bouillon cubes
4 Irish potatoes, diced
3 carrots, sliced
3 celery stalks, diced
1 large green bell pepper, diced
1 medium onion, diced
1 bay leaf

PREP TIME: 30 minutes

COOK TIME: 4 to 8 hours

PER SERVING: Calories: 311; Total fat: 10g;
Saturated fat: 1g; Cholesterol: 0mg; Carbs: 26g;
Fiber: 3g; Protein: 28g; Sodium: 1343mg

1. Put the stew meat in a gallon-size freezer bag. Add the flour, 1 teaspoon of salt, and the pepper. Seal the bag and toss to coat.

2. In a large skillet over medium heat, heat the vegetable oil.

3. Add the meat. Cook for 10 to 12 minutes, stirring often, until browned. Transfer the browned meat to a slow cooker and add the water.

4. Stir in the remaining 3 teaspoons of salt and the beef bouillon cubes.

5. Add the potatoes, carrots, celery, bell pepper, onion, and bay leaf.

6. Cover the pot and cook for 4 hours on high or 8 hours on low, until the meat and vegetables are tender.

GLUTEN-FREE OPTION: Use gluten-free all-purpose flour.

INGREDIENT TIP: If you don't have beef stew meat, substitute a 2-pound roast, cut into 1-inch pieces.

TIME-SAVING TIP: Use 1 cup of frozen bell pepper and onion blend instead of fresh peppers and onions.

MY DAD'S FAVORITE CHILI

DF | **NF**

Heirloom Recipe | SERVES **6**

My dad didn't cook often, *for which the entire family was thankful.* Whenever he tried to cook, the meal was usually burnt or tasted so bad I would skip it and forage for something later. As he got older and had grandchildren who also complained about his cooking, he finally got the message and reduced his menu to three items the entire family would eat—cheesy scrambled eggs, pinto beans, and chili. On cold winter evenings, we'd gather around the dining room table to eat this thick, meaty chili with a side of corn bread. Whenever I make this chili, I'm reminded of his one meal from my childhood that didn't earn an "ick."

2 pounds ground beef

4 garlic cloves, minced

½ medium yellow onion, chopped

4 bay leaves

1 teaspoon salt

1 teaspoon freshly ground
    black pepper

1 (6-ounce) can tomato paste

4 tablespoons chili powder

2 tablespoons all-purpose flour

1 teaspoon ground cumin

1 teaspoon dried thyme

1 (15-ounce) can pinto beans, rinsed
    and drained

1 (15-ounce) kidney beans or black
    beans, rinsed and drained

½ to 1 cup water

PREP TIME: 20 minutes

COOK TIME: 25 minutes

PER SERVING: Calories: 412; Total fat: 13g; Saturated fat: 4g; Cholesterol: 93mg; Carbs: 38g; Fiber: 12g; Protein: 40g; Sodium: 1036mg

1. In a medium skillet over medium heat, combine the ground beef, garlic, onion, and bay leaves. Cook the beef for about 10 minutes, breaking it up with the back of a spoon, until browned. Drain the beef mixture. Stir in the salt and pepper, and set it aside.

2. In a medium bowl, stir together the tomato paste, chili powder, flour, cumin, and thyme.

3. Put the pinto and kidney beans in a stockpot.

4. Add the ground beef mixture and the tomato mixture and stir until combined.

5. Slowly add the water until the desired thickness is reached. Use less water for a thicker chili and more for a thinner chili. Turn the heat to high and bring the mixture to a boil. Reduce the heat to low and simmer the chili for 10 minutes. Remove and discard the bay leaves before serving.

HOW-TO TIP: To dry your own herbs, place one paper towel in the microwave. Arrange 4 stems of herbs on top of the paper towel, spreading them out so they do not touch. Place another paper towel on top of the herbs. Microwave for 2 minutes on 100 percent power. If not completely dried, microwave for 1 minute more.

VARIATION TIP: Want to add a flavor twist? Use ½ cup strong black coffee instead of the water.

GLUTEN-FREE OPTION: Use gluten-free all-purpose flour.

FRIED CHICKEN page 80

Six

FLY THE COOP

—

CHICKEN

BRITTANY Dad and I like to joke that we could give Mom a pack of hamburger meat and still wind up having chicken for supper. It's her favorite protein, and it's graced our dinner table in a thousand forms. Although fried chicken is synonymous with Southern cooking—and don't get me wrong, we love it—we're just as likely to have a chicken casserole as a chicken leg. And if we go out to the local meat and three for a quick lunch? Well, Mom's just got to order the chicken and dressing. It was one of my mom's proudest moments when my daughter learned to talk and "chicken" was one of her first words. Jenna's favorite way to eat it is still in nugget form, but armed with all the chicken recipes here, we have hope we can change that over time.

FRIED CHICKEN
(PLUS BAKED "FRIED" VERSION)

NF | *Heirloom Recipe* | SERVES **8**

Fried chicken is classic Southern food. No matter the event—potluck, tailgate, church dinner, or funeral—someone brings a platter filled to the brim with fried chicken. When my father-in-law died, our church brought an "after the funeral meal" to our house for the family. There were 15 of us and four pounds of fried chicken. Before everyone had gotten their food, all the fried chicken was gone. The rest of us had glazed ham.

Everyone has a preference. Crispy or not, buttermilk battered or egg battered, cornmeal or flour breaded. It's a hotly debated topic. Although I usually serve only baked "fried" chicken now (see variation tip), my favorite chicken is the kind I watched my aunts prepare: dipped in milk and fried to a crispy golden brown.

1 cup sifted all-purpose flour

1 teaspoon salt

1 teaspoon sugar

½ teaspoon paprika

¼ teaspoon freshly ground black pepper

1 large egg, slightly beaten

1 cup whole milk (see ingredient tip)

1½ cups cooking oil (corn, vegetable, or canola)

1 (3- to 4-pound) whole broiler/fryer chicken, cut into pieces, skin removed (see ingredient tip)

PREP TIME: 10 minutes, plus 10 minutes sitting time

COOK TIME: 45 minutes

PER SERVING: Calories: 287; Total fat: 13g; Saturated fat: 3g; Cholesterol: 110mg; Carbs: 14g; Fiber: 1g; Protein: 28g; Sodium: 466mg

1. In a medium bowl, stir together the flour, salt, sugar, paprika, and pepper until blended.

2. In a small bowl, whisk the egg and milk. Add this to the flour mixture, whisk to combine, and let sit for 10 minutes.

3. In a cast iron skillet over medium heat, heat the cooking oil until it shimmers. You'll have enough chicken that you might have to use two skillets, or fry the chicken in two batches.

4. Dip the chicken pieces into the batter and let any excess drain back into the bowl.

5. Carefully add the battered chicken to the hot oil. Cook for 10 minutes. Flip and cook for 8 minutes more, until browned.

6. Once all the chicken is browned, lower the heat to medium-low. Cover the skillet and cook the chicken for 25 minutes or until tender.

INGREDIENT TIP: Four pounds skinless chicken legs or thighs can be substituted for the whole chicken. Buttermilk can be substituted for the whole milk.

VARIATION TIP: Make it baked "fried" chicken: Preheat the oven to 350°F and coat a casserole dish with nonstick cooking spray. Prepare the flour mixture and coat the chicken as directed. Place the chicken in the prepared casserole dish. Cover with aluminum foil. Bake for 30 to 40 minutes or until the chicken is no longer pink inside.

GLUTEN-FREE OPTION: Use gluten-free all-purpose flour.

"GROWING UP SOUTHERN IS A PRIVILEGE, REALLY. IT'S MORE THAN WHERE YOU'RE BORN, IT'S AN IDEA AND STATE OF MIND THAT SEEMS IMPARTED AT BIRTH. IT'S MORE THAN LOVING FRIED CHICKEN, SWEET TEA, AND COUNTRY SONGS. IT'S BEING HOSPITABLE, DEVOTED TO FRONT PORCHES, MOON PIES, SUN DROP . . . AND EACH OTHER. WE DON'T BECOME SOUTHERN— WE'RE BORN THAT WAY."

—UNKNOWN

CHICKEN AND CHEDDAR DUMPLINGS

NF *Heirloom Recipe* | SERVES **8**

My Aunt Kay was the kind of aunt all little girls dream of having—soft-spoken and kind to everyone. She was an expert at many things, from sewing to gardening. But her cooking! It was to die for. All the nieces and nephews eagerly awaited her arrival at family dinners, carrying a wash pan full of food, with another following in my Uncle Hermit's arms. We'd gather around the food as soon as she sat it on the kitchen table and pepper her with questions. "Did you bring your tea cakes? What about your spaghetti? I want fried catfish! Is this slaw and hushpuppies?" One dish we could always count on was her chicken and dumplings. We adapted her recipe to include Cheddar dumplings instead of the traditional ones, but I'm sure Aunt Kay would approve.

FOR THE CHICKEN

1 tablespoon poultry seasoning

2 teaspoons salt

1 bay leaf

2 quarts chicken broth

2 quarts water

1 whole (3- to 4-pound) fryer/
 roaster chicken

3 carrots, sliced

3 celery stalks, chopped

1 medium yellow onion, diced

FOR THE DUMPLINGS

¾ cup shortening

3 cups all-purpose flour

½ cup shredded sharp Cheddar
 cheese (optional)

¾ cup whole or 2% milk

GLUTEN-FREE OPTION: Use gluten-free all-purpose flour.

PREP TIME: 40 minutes

COOK TIME: 2 hours, 30 minutes

PER SERVING: Calories: 532; Total fat: 26g; Saturated fat: 8g; Cholesterol: 81mg; Carbs: 40g; Fiber: 2g; Protein: 34g; Sodium: 911mg

TO MAKE THE CHICKEN

1. In a small bowl, combine the poultry seasoning, salt, and bay leaf.

2. In a large bowl, stir together the chicken broth and water. Stir in the poultry seasoning mixture.

3. Place the chicken in a large stockpot with the carrots, celery, and onion.

4. Pour the chicken broth mixture over the chicken and vegetables. Turn the heat to medium-high and bring the mixture to a boil. Cover the pot, reduce the heat to medium-low, and simmer for 2 hours.

5. Remove the chicken from the pot and let it cool briefly. Remove the meat from the bones and cut it into pieces.

6. Strain the broth and return it to the pot.

TO MAKE THE DUMPLINGS

1. In a medium bowl, use your fingertips or a pastry cutter to cut the shortening into the flour until crumbs form.

2. Add the cheese to the crumbs (if using).

3. Add the milk. Stir until the mixture forms a ball.

4. Lightly flour a work surface and place the dumpling dough on it. Knead for about 4 minutes, until smooth, not sticky, like biscuit dough. Roll out the dough until it is about ⅛ inch thick. Cut it into 1-inch squares.

5. Bring the strained chicken broth to a rapid boil over high heat. Drop the dumplings into the boiling broth. Let everything return to a rapid boil. Lower the heat to medium-low and simmer for 10 minutes.

6. Add the chicken pieces and simmer for 10 minutes more.

7. Remove from the heat and let the chicken and dumplings sit for 10 minutes before serving.

CHICKEN IN LEMON CREAM SAUCE

GF | **NF**

New Favorite | SERVES **3** TO **4**

When I graduated college, the first thing I did was shop for a new car. While shopping for said car, I browsed through a cookbook at one of the auto dealers and ended up purchasing a copy. Needing cooking inspiration one afternoon, I found a recipe called Chicken with Lime Butter. It looked good, but I never leave recipes alone. I adapt them with whatever is in the fridge or pantry that catches my eye. I ignored the original ingredients and added mushrooms, lemon juice, cream, and Parmesan. I make this when I need a special-occasion meal but don't want to spend a lot of time in the kitchen.

3 boneless, skinless chicken breasts

½ teaspoon salt

½ teaspoon freshly ground black pepper

⅓ cup salted butter

1 (8-ounce) package mushrooms, sliced

1 cup heavy (whipping) cream

½ cup freshly squeezed lemon juice

1 tablespoon minced fresh chives

¼ cup shredded Parmesan cheese

PREP TIME: 10 minutes

COOK TIME: 25 minutes

PER SERVING: Calories: 632; Total fat: 54g; Saturated fat: 33g; Cholesterol: 235mg; Carbs: 6g; Fiber: 1g; Protein: 34g; Sodium: 737mg

1. Sprinkle the chicken breasts with the salt and pepper.

2. In a skillet over medium heat, melt the butter.

3. Add the chicken. Cook for 3 minutes, turn, and cook for 3 minutes more.

4. Add the mushrooms, cream, and lemon juice. Turn the heat to medium-low and cover the skillet. Simmer for 15 to 20 minutes, turning occasionally, until the chicken is cooked through and the juices run clear.

5. Sprinkle the chicken with the chives and Parmesan before serving.

INGREDIENT TIP: When cooking dishes with cream, like this one, be sure to use heavy (whipping) cream. It's less likely to curdle during cooking. Don't have any heavy cream? Substitute ¾ cup of whole milk and ¼ cup of melted butter for 1 cup of cream. This substitute, however, cannot be made into whipped cream.

BAKED CHICKEN SALAD

GF | *Updated Classic* | SERVES **6**

As a preteen, I volunteered during the summer at the local library with my best friend. The librarian of the children's section was the mom of my crush, and she harbored a secret hope that her son and I would fall deeply in love and get married. *That didn't work out*, but she had a soft spot for my friend and me. Some days, she would press a $20 bill into our hands and tell us to go find some lunch. It was a small town—we only had one red light—and there were only two restaurants. When we wanted something a little fancy, we would visit Nanny at the bank where she worked and change into dresses. Then we'd walk over to the fancy tearoom and order chicken salad, pimento cheese, and raspberry iced tea. This baked chicken salad is a twist on that old favorite. Served warm, this chicken salad is extra creamy with melted cheese, but the almonds give it a delicious crunch.

Nonstick cooking spray

4 celery stalks, thinly sliced

1 medium yellow onion, minced

2 cups mayonnaise

½ cup sliced almonds, toasted (see how-to tip)

2 tablespoons freshly squeezed lemon juice

2 cups diced cooked chicken

½ teaspoon salt

¾ cup grated sharp Cheddar cheese

Gluten-free crackers (we like Milton's brand) or lettuce leaves, for serving

PREP TIME: 25 minutes

COOK TIME: 15 minutes

PER SERVING: Calories: 489; Total fat: 36g; Saturated fat: 8g; Cholesterol: 71mg; Carbs: 23g; Fiber: 2g; Protein: 20g; Sodium: 879mg

1. Preheat the oven to 450°F. Coat a 2-quart casserole dish with cooking spray, and set it aside.

2. In a large bowl, stir together the celery, onion, mayonnaise, almonds, and lemon juice.

3. Add the chicken and salt and stir to coat in the mayonnaise. Pour the chicken mixture into the prepared casserole dish.

4. Sprinkle the cheese evenly over the casserole.

5. Bake for 15 minutes. Serve warm with gluten-free toast or crackers, or scoop it into lettuce leaves.

HOW-TO TIP: To toast almonds (or other nuts), preheat the oven to 350°F. Spread the almond slices evenly on a baking sheet. Bake for 3 to 4 minutes, until toasty and fragrant. Let cool.

CHICKEN AND CORN BREAD DRESSING

Brittany's Recipe

NF | *Heirloom Recipe* | SERVES **12**

If I could choose a last meal, it would be this chicken and dressing. While most of my family is partial to stuffing (*yuck*), I've always been a dressing fan. Now, in some parts of the country, these are the same thing—except stuffing goes inside the turkey and dressing is cooked separately. Some of my friends always fight me on this. But down here? Dressing and stuffing are two different things. Stuffing is made of white bread and generally is chunky. Dressing is made of corn bread and comes in loaf form. It's topped with a gravy that has meat in it. As you'll see, *dressing is obviously the superior choice.*

FOR THE CORN BREAD DRESSING

Nonstick cooking spray

4 cups crumbled corn bread (see Broccoli Corn Bread variation, page 13)

1½ cups crumbled bread (I use French bread)

1 quart chicken broth, divided

2 celery stalks, chopped

1 medium yellow onion, chopped

1 tablespoon dried sage

½ teaspoon freshly ground black pepper

3 large eggs, beaten

FOR THE CHICKEN GRAVY

1 tablespoon all-purpose flour

½ teaspoon salt

½ teaspoon freshly ground black pepper

½ teaspoon dried sage

2 cups chicken broth

¼ cup water

2½ cups shredded boiled or baked chicken

2 large hard-boiled eggs, peeled and diced

PREP TIME: 30 minutes

COOK TIME: 40 minutes

PER SERVING: Calories: 234; Total fat: 7g; Saturated fat: 2g; Cholesterol: 113mg; Carbs: 26g; Fiber: 1g; Protein: 17g; Sodium: 714mg

TO MAKE THE CORN BREAD DRESSING

1. Preheat the oven to 450°F. Coat a 9-by-13-inch baking dish with cooking spray, and set it aside.

2. In a large bowl, stir together the corn bread and bread. Set aside.

3. In a medium skillet over medium heat, combine ¼ cup of chicken broth, the celery, onion, sage, and pepper. Cook for 5 to 7 minutes, until the vegetables are tender.

4. Add this to the corn bread mixture, along with the eggs. Stir to combine.

5. Add the remaining 1¾ cups of chicken broth and stir. The mixture will be soupy! Pour the dressing into the prepared baking dish. Bake for 30 minutes.

TO MAKE THE CHICKEN GRAVY

1. In a small bowl, stir together the flour, salt, pepper, and sage.

2. In a medium saucepan, combine the chicken broth and water. Stir in the flour mixture. Place the pan over medium heat. Cook for 5 to 10 minutes, until the gravy thickens.

3. Stir in the chicken and diced eggs.

4. Serve the corn bread dressing with the chicken gravy on top.

INGREDIENT TIP: Have leftover turkey but no chicken? Substitute an equal amount of turkey for the chicken in this recipe. An equal amount of turkey broth can be substituted for the chicken broth.

MAKE-AHEAD TIP: Make the dressing and freeze it for up to 2 months before baking. Thaw it in the refrigerator for 24 hours. Let stand at room temperature for 30 minutes before baking as directed.

"THE BEST COMFORT FOOD WILL ALWAYS BE GREENS, CORNBREAD, AND FRIED CHICKEN."

—MAYA ANGELOU

CHICKEN CASSEROLE

NF

Updated Classic | SERVES **8**

Chicken casseroles are synonymous with life in the South, and every family has a recipe that's been passed down for generations—and every family swears theirs is the best. If there's a potluck after Sunday church, you can guarantee there are at least *six types* of chicken casserole on the buffet. And if there's a holiday my family celebrates? Well, there's a chicken casserole there as well.

I'm not sure why my grandmother decided our family gatherings needed casserole, but we've always been glad she did. We look forward to diving into that rich, buttery casserole *(and ours is pretty special because the sauce is from scratch, not some canned soup)* just as much as we look forward to opening our Christmas presents. If there are any leftovers, warm them up for lunch the next day . . . or eat them cold for breakfast. We won't tell.

FOR THE CHICKEN

4 boneless, skinless chicken breasts

FOR THE SAUCE

2 tablespoons salted butter
2 tablespoons all-purpose flour
1 cup whole milk
½ cup sliced mushrooms
1 teaspoon salt
1 teaspoon freshly ground
    black pepper

PREP TIME: 45 minutes

COOK TIME: 50 minutes

PER SERVING: Calories: 398; Total fat: 28g;
Saturated fat: 16g; Cholesterol: 99mg; Carbs: 16g;
Fiber: 1g; Protein: 22g; Sodium: 720mg

FOR THE CASSEROLE

1 cup sour cream
½ cup chicken stock (reserved from
    cooking the chicken)
½ cup shredded Parmesan cheese
1 tablespoon freshly squeezed
    lemon juice
1 tablespoon white wine
1½ teaspoons Italian seasoning
1 tablespoon poppy seeds

FOR THE TOPPING

1 sleeve butter-flavored
    crackers, crushed
8 tablespoons (1 stick) salted butter

TO MAKE THE CHICKEN

1. Place the chicken breasts in a medium saucepan and cover with water. Bring to a boil and cook until tender, about 20 minutes. Reserve ½ cup of the cooking water.

2. Dice the chicken and set it aside.

TO MAKE THE SAUCE

1. In a nonstick skillet over medium heat, melt the butter.

2. Add the flour. Stir until combined.

3. Add the milk. Cook for about 5 minutes, stirring, until thickened.

4. Add the mushrooms. Simmer for 5 minutes.

5. Season with the salt and pepper.

TO MAKE THE CASSEROLE

1. Preheat the oven to 350°F.

2. To the sauce, add the sour cream, reserved chicken stock, Parmesan, lemon juice, white wine, and Italian seasoning. Stir until blended.

3. Stir in the chicken. Spread the casserole evenly in a 2-quart casserole dish.

4. Sprinkle the poppy seeds evenly over the top.

TO MAKE THE TOPPING

1. In a small bowl, stir together the crushed crackers and melted butter until blended. Spread the topping evenly over the casserole.

2. Bake for 30 minutes, until bubbly.

HOW-TO TIP: A roux is made of fat (often butter) and flour and is used to thicken sauces. In this dish, we make a simple white roux, which thickens the sauce without influencing the flavor.

TIME-SAVING TIP: Four cups of left-over diced cooked chicken can be used instead of boiling the chicken breasts.

GLUTEN-FREE OPTION: Substitute gluten-free all-purpose flour and omit the cracker topping.

HERBED BAKED CHICKEN WITH TANGY ORANGE SAUCE

NF

Updated Classic | SERVES **4**

Every summer, I looked forward to the two weeks my Aunt Inez and Cousin Teresa would come to visit my grandmother. They lived 600 miles away, and we saw them only once a year. My aunt, a home economics teacher, would arrive with sacks full of groceries to prepare meals I didn't have any other time of the year. She'd plan the weekly menus, just as she did at home, and sometimes, when we were young teenagers, she would send us to the store to pick up an ingredient. This was an adventure because the store was a mile away and we weren't old enough to drive. Rather than walk, *we'd take the tractor.* My cousin, who was the eldest and made sure I never forgot that fact, drove, while I sat on the wheel hub. When I began to cook, I'd ask Inez for her recipes. Later, I made adaptions for my family's tastes, like this recipe. We serve it with this simple, tangy orange sauce for dipping.

FOR THE CHICKEN

¼ cup all-purpose flour

¼ teaspoon dried oregano

¼ teaspoon dried thyme

¼ teaspoon garlic powder

¼ teaspoon salt

¼ teaspoon freshly ground
    black pepper

4 boneless, skinless chicken breasts

8 tablespoons (1 stick) salted
    butter, melted

4 teaspoons chopped fresh
    chives, divided

¼ cup grated Parmesan cheese, divided

FOR THE DIPPING SAUCE

1 tablespoon orange juice

1 tablespoon honey

1 tablespoon soy sauce

PREP TIME: 15 minutes

COOK TIME: 20 to 25 minutes

PER SERVING: Calories: 426; Total fat: 27g;
Saturated fat: 16g; Cholesterol: 147mg; Carbs: 12g;
Fiber: 0g; Protein: 36g; Sodium: 696mg

TO MAKE THE CHICKEN

1. Preheat the oven to 450°F.

2. In a gallon-size freezer bag, combine the flour, oregano, thyme, garlic powder, salt, and pepper.

3. Add the chicken, seal the bag, and shake until the chicken is covered. Place the coated chicken in a 2-quart baking dish. Pour the melted butter evenly over the chicken.

4. Bake for 20 to 25 minutes, or until the chicken is no longer pink.

TO MAKE THE DIPPING SAUCE

1. While the chicken is baking, combine the orange juice, honey, and soy sauce, and stir until blended.

2. Remove the chicken from the oven and sprinkle each piece with 1 teaspoon of chives and 1 tablespoon of Parmesan. Serve with the tangy orange dipping sauce.

HOW-TO TIP: Save money by purchasing a block of Parmesan cheese. Cut the cheese into ½-inch chunks and place them in the food processor. Process with the regular blade for 1 to 2 minutes, until finely "grated."

GLUTEN-FREE OPTION: Use gluten-free all-purpose flour.

CHEESY BAKED CHICKEN STRIPS

| NF | | *New Favorite* | SERVES **4** |

When I was young, our neighbors moved to Nashville, Tennessee. We had been friends with them for several years, so when the chance arose, we packed our bags and went visiting. After a fun-filled day at a local water park, we stopped at a popular (and pricey) barbecue joint. I wasn't in the mood for barbecue, so I ordered chicken strips. As soon as they arrived, I knew I had made a mistake. "I can't eat these," I said. Our exasperated neighbor asked, "Why can't you eat your $8 chicken strips?" "They're fried! I don't want fried chicken. Mom bakes her chicken tenders so they're healthier. That's what I want." *I'm pretty sure she rolled her eyes.* That was years ago, but this is still the recipe I think of when I want chicken strips. The cheese really makes the flavor pop, and I like mine with this honey mustard dipping sauce.

FOR THE CHICKEN

Nonstick cooking spray

3 large eggs, beaten

6 slices bread (your choice; I use French bread)

1 tablespoon Italian seasoning

½ teaspoon salt

½ teaspoon freshly ground black pepper

1 cup shredded sharp Cheddar cheese

1 pound boneless, skinless chicken breasts, cut into strips about 1 inch wide

FOR THE DIPPING SAUCE

½ cup mayonnaise

¼ cup Dijon mustard

¼ cup honey

¼ teaspoon garlic salt

PREP TIME: 20 minutes

COOK TIME: 20 minutes

PER SERVING: Calories: 556; Total fat: 26g; Saturated fat: 9g; Cholesterol: 259mg; Carbs: 34g; Fiber: 1g; Protein: 45g; Sodium: 1089mg

TO MAKE THE CHICKEN

1. Preheat the oven to 350°F. Spray a baking sheet with cooking spray, and set it aside.

2. Place the beaten eggs in a shallow bowl.

3. In a food processor fitted with the standard blade, chop the bread for 15 to 20 seconds to make crumbs. Add the Italian seasoning, salt, pepper, and cheese. Pulse to combine. Transfer the crumb mixture to a shallow bowl.

4. Using a fork, dredge the chicken strips, one at a time, first in the egg mixture and then in the crumb mixture, coating both sides evenly. Place the coated chicken strips on the prepared baking sheet.

5. Bake for 20 minutes, turning the chicken after 10 minutes, until golden brown and cooked through.

TO MAKE THE DIPPING SAUCE

While the chicken cooks, mix together the mayonnaise, mustard, honey, and garlic salt. Serve the chicken with the dipping sauce.

DID YOU KNOW?: Chickens accompanied Roman soldiers to war. If the chickens had a good appetite before the battle, it was believed the Romans would be victorious.

DAIRY-FREE OPTION: Substitute shredded vegan cheese or nutritional yeast for the Cheddar.

GLUTEN-FREE OPTION: Use gluten-free bread.

CHICKEN POTPIE WITH CORNMEAL PASTRY

NF

Updated Classic | SERVES **6**

My Grandmother Perry raised chickens. *I'm not sure why.* We didn't eat them. These were free-range chickens, so they wandered off to lay their eggs, leaving us unable to find them. I had no problem with these chickens—except the rooster. This rooster was the bane of my existence! On weekends or in summer, I wanted to sleep late. The rooster, a cocky little bantam with a crow that could wake the dead, had other ideas. No matter which bedroom I used, this rooster sensed where I was. He would come each morning at 5 a.m. to stand under my window and crow. *Loudly.* Nothing deterred him—not yelling or the occasional shoe thrown out the window. I spent a lot of mornings threatening to make him into potpie. It was an idle threat, and he lived to a ripe old age. But if I had made good on my threat, this is the recipe I would have used, which has been updated with a cornmeal crust.

FOR THE FILLING

Nonstick cooking spray

3 cups diced cooked chicken

2 carrots, cooked and sliced

2 Irish potatoes, diced

1 small yellow onion, diced

½ cup cooked green peas

4 tablespoons (½ stick) salted
    butter, melted

¼ cup all-purpose flour

1 teaspoon salt

1 teaspoon poultry seasoning (see
    how-to tip)

½ teaspoon freshly ground
    black pepper

2½ cups chicken broth

PREP TIME: 30 minutes

COOK TIME: 40 minutes

FOR THE CORNMEAL PASTRY

¾ cup all-purpose flour

½ cup cornmeal

¾ teaspoon salt

⅓ cup vegetable shortening

3 tablespoons water

PER SERVING: Calories: 476; Total fat: 23g; Saturated fat: 9g; Cholesterol: 74mg; Carbs: 40g; Fiber: 5g; Protein: 28g; Sodium: 918mg

TO MAKE THE FILLING

1. Spray a 2-quart casserole dish with cooking spray. Put the chicken, carrots, potatoes, onion, and green peas in the dish. Stir to combine, and set it aside.

2. In a nonstick skillet over medium heat, melt the butter.

3. Stir in the flour, salt, poultry seasoning, and pepper until blended.

4. Gradually add the chicken broth, stirring constantly. Cook for 5 to 10 minutes, until the mixture thickens. Pour the chicken broth over the chicken and vegetables.

TO MAKE THE CORNMEAL PASTRY

1. Preheat the oven to 400°F.

2. In a medium bowl, stir together the flour, cornmeal, and salt.

3. Add the shortening. Use your fingertips or a pastry cutter to cut the shortening into the dry ingredients until the mixture makes crumbs.

4. Add the water, 1 tablespoon at a time, mixing after each addition. Shape the dough into a ball. Roll out the dough to an ⅛-inch thickness. Top the chicken filling with the pastry. Cut slits in the top for steam to escape.

5. Bake for 25 to 30 minutes, until the top is light brown and the filling is bubbling.

HOW-TO TIP: To make your own poultry seasoning, mix together the following dried spices: 4 teaspoons ground sage, 3 teaspoons ground thyme, 2 teaspoons ground marjoram, 1½ teaspoons ground rosemary, 1 teaspoon freshly ground black pepper, and 1 teaspoon ground nutmeg.

DAIRY-FREE OPTION: Use vegan butter.

GLUTEN-FREE OPTION: Use gluten-free all-purpose flour.

BRITTANY AND TAYLOR'S BIRTHDAY DESSERT

When Brittany was 10, she and her best friend, Taylor, decided they wanted to learn to cook. Taylor lived one street over, so they were able to spend as much time together as they wanted. Unfortunately, their cooking skills left a lot to be desired, due to their tendency to deviate from a recipe and add "unusual" ingredients.

On my birthday, they treated me to a special birthday dinner they made "all by themselves." It consisted of their "Spaghetti Exotica," which was spaghetti with (almost) every spice in my cabinet, and a mystery dessert that included a twist tie in the center because they couldn't find a candle. I thanked them, wondering how many bites I had to eat before I could politely say I was full. "Don't forget to share your dessert with us, Miss Pam!" Taylor said. "Believe me, I won't," I said, pushing it toward them. They both took a bite. "Hmmmm," Taylor said, glancing toward me. "This isn't as bad as I thought it would be!" I've had lots of birthday desserts, but this one will stand out in my memory forever. And while it wasn't good, it wasn't as bad as I thought it would be, either.

—Pam

OVEN-BARBECUED CHICKEN WITH ALABAMA WHITE SAUCE

DF | GF | NF

New Favorite | SERVES **4**

We take our barbecue seriously in the South. Every state has their own style, and they all think it's the best. North Carolina has a tangy, vinegar-based sauce, while South Carolina has a mustard-based sauce. In Texas, you'll find a basting sauce, but in Alabama, you'll find a white, mayonnaise-based barbecue sauce. I first discovered this sauce when my husband, Bryan, worked in Birmingham. He spent two weeks each month out of town, and we visited as often as we could. One day, the kids were "so starved" when we arrived, so we stopped by the Tin Roof BBQ for dinner. The waitress asked, "What kind of sauce do you want, y'all?" and pulled out a bottle of white sauce. *I was hooked.* Whenever we visited, I pushed away all other sauces and grabbed the white sauce. We live three and a half hours away from Birmingham now, and Tin Roof has sadly closed, so I had to re-create my own.

4 boneless, skinless chicken breasts

¾ cup mayonnaise

½ cup sugar

6 tablespoons white vinegar

6 tablespoons freshly squeezed
  lemon juice

1½ teaspoons salt

1 teaspoon freshly ground
  black pepper

8 drops hot sauce (I use Tabasco)

1. Preheat the oven to 350°F.

2. Place the chicken breasts in a 2-quart casserole dish.

3. In a small bowl, stir together the mayonnaise, sugar, vinegar, lemon juice, salt, pepper, and hot sauce until blended. Pour the sauce evenly over the chicken.

4. Bake for 20 to 25 minutes, or until the chicken is no longer pink.

PREP TIME: 15 minutes

COOK TIME: 20 to 25 minutes

PER SERVING: Calories: 452; Total fat: 20g; Saturated fat: 4g; Cholesterol: 93mg; Carbs: 37g; Fiber: 0g; Protein: 32g; Sodium: 941mg

DID YOU KNOW?: Roosters like to impress hens by tidbitting. The rooster makes noises, picks up and drops food, and moves its head, hoping to attract the hens to his side.

HONEY BARBECUE WINGS WITH PEACH SWEET 'N' SOUR SAUCE

DF | **NF**

New Favorite | SERVES **4**

We have four seasons here in the South: *winter, pollen, tornado, and football.* The Southeastern Conference (SEC) is practically a religion in some households. While our family isn't *as* into football as some families we know, we absolutely love a good tailgate. I may not know exactly what a touchdown is, but I know for sure which of my friends' moms makes the best refreshments. At any tailgate, there must be wings. It's basically the law. These honey barbecue wings are always our answer when someone asks, "What are y'all bringing to the tailgate?" The touch of honey instead of a traditional barbeque sauce gives them a flavor almost everyone will love. Serve them with the peach sweet 'n' sour dipping sauce, and you're sure to win the tailgate.

FOR THE WINGS

1 cup honey

½ cup ketchup

½ cup soy sauce

2 tablespoons vegetable oil

2 tablespoons minced garlic

2 tablespoons chopped fresh chives

½ teaspoon freshly ground
    black pepper

20 chicken wings

PREP TIME: 15 minutes, plus 30 minutes marinating time

COOK TIME: 1 hour, 15 minutes

PER SERVING: Calories: 819; Total fat: 30g; Saturated fat: 7g; Cholesterol: 112mg; Carbs: 113g; Fiber: 1g; Protein: 31g; Sodium: 2137mg

FOR THE DIPPING SAUCE

1 cup chopped canned peaches or
    1 cup peeled and chopped fresh
    peaches (about 1½)

½ cup sugar

½ cup white vinegar

1½ tablespoons cornstarch

¼ cup water

TO MAKE THE WINGS

1. In a small bowl, whisk the honey, ketchup, soy sauce, vegetable oil, garlic, chives, and pepper until blended.

2. In a gallon-size freezer bag, combine the wings and marinade. Seal the bag and refrigerate to marinate for 30 minutes.

3. Preheat the oven to 375°F.

4. Transfer the wings and the marinade to a 3-quart baking dish.

5. Bake for 1 hour, 15 minutes, or until the wings are brown, checking them occasionally and basting as necessary.

TO MAKE THE DIPPING SAUCE

1. While the wings are baking, prepare the dipping sauce. Mash the peaches—if using canned, mash them with some of their juice.

2. Combine the peaches, sugar, and white vinegar in a saucepan. Cook over medium heat until the sugar has dissolved.

3. In a small bowl, mix the cornstarch and water until blended. Add the cornstarch mixture to the peach mixture and stir until it simmers. Stir constantly for about 1 minute or until the mixture thickens slightly. Serve the wings with the dipping sauce.

HOW-TO TIP: If your honey has crystalized, place the jar or bottle in a bowl of warm water and let it warm. Stir before using.

GLUTEN-FREE OPTION: Use gluten-free soy sauce (tamari).

"GOOD FOOD IS ALL THE SWEETER WHEN SHARED WITH GOOD FRIENDS."

—SOUTHERN SAYING

PAM'S CHICKEN WITH ARTICHOKES

NF | *New Favorite* | SERVES **4**

Chicken is my favorite meat, so we have it often. I didn't realize how often until one day, when I asked my husband, Bryan, "What should I do with this chicken tonight?" He mumbled under his breath, "Throw it in the garbage." That's when I decided I needed some new chicken recipes. Since I'm all about easy and not running to the store for ingredients, I searched my pantry and fridge. Guess what I found? Leftovers.

I'm not going to lie. *My family hates leftovers.* I'm constantly looking for sneaky ways to use them. This dish is great because it uses leftover cooked chicken and leftover noodles. My son, Ashton, asked me, "Are you sure this dish is Southern?" I told him, "We live in the South and we're eating it. That makes it Southern." Maybe my grandparents didn't have artichoke hearts, but if they had, this would have been on their menu.

2 cups cubed cooked chicken
1 (6-ounce) jar artichoke hearts, drained and chopped
2 cups cooked egg noodles
½ cup heavy (whipping) cream or whole milk
½ cup shredded Parmesan cheese

PREP TIME: 10 minutes

COOK TIME: 10 minutes

PER SERVING: Calories: 439; Total fat: 24g; Saturated fat: 11g; Cholesterol: 128mg; Carbs: 24g; Fiber: 1g; Protein: 29g; Sodium: 327mg

GLUTEN-FREE OPTION: Use gluten-free egg noodles.

DAIRY-FREE OPTION: Substitute soy milk and use vegan cheese.

1. In a medium skillet over medium heat, combine the chicken, artichoke hearts, egg noodles, and cream. Cook for 5 to 10 minutes, stirring constantly, until heated through.

2. Sprinkle with the Parmesan and serve.

MAKE-AHEAD TIP: Purchase a 4-pound package of boneless, skinless chicken breasts. Place them in a large saucepan and cover with water. Cook for 20 to 25 minutes or until the chicken is done. Cube, shred, or slice the chicken. Divide it into four portions and place each portion in a freezer bag. Freeze. Thaw in the fridge before use.

PESTO CHICKEN

Updated Classic | SERVES **6**

Our family has always had a garden of some sort. No matter what else we plant—like 50 acres of watermelons—Mom always grows a yard full of herbs. *Pam's note: That's an exaggeration, Brittany! My dad planted seven acres of watermelons. I never knew why.*

Some years we have exotic herbs, like pineapple mint. Some years we stick with the basics. But every year, Mom plants basil. I don't know what she does, because I can never grow basil, but hers always thrives under her loving attention. And every year, when the basil is as big as a boxwood bush, Mom tears off leaves to make pesto. As a child, I waited patiently for pesto season. When it finally came around, I ate nothing but sandwiches of brown bread with this pesto and homegrown tomatoes. We use almonds instead of pine nuts, due to allergies, but feel free to substitute an equal amount of pine nuts instead.

4 cups fresh basil leaves

½ cup shredded Parmesan cheese, plus more for garnishing (optional)

¼ cup almonds, toasted (see how-to tip on page 85) and chopped

1 tablespoon minced garlic

½ cup olive oil

1 teaspoon salt

1 (16-ounce) box penne pasta

2 cups shredded cooked chicken

PREP TIME: 15 minutes

COOK TIME: 15 minutes

PER SERVING: Calories: 470; Total fat: 23g; Saturated fat: 4g; Cholesterol: 43mg; Carbs: 44g; Fiber: 3g; Protein: 25g; Sodium: 504mg

GLUTEN-FREE OPTION: Use gluten-free penne.

1. In a food processor fitted with the standard blade, combine the basil, Parmesan, almonds, and garlic. With the processor running, slowly add the olive oil, blending until the pesto is puréed. Season to taste with the salt. Process again to combine. Set aside.

2. Cook the pasta according to the package directions. Drain and transfer to a large bowl.

3. Add the pesto and cooked chicken. Toss to coat and combine.

4. Garnish with Parmesan (if using).

DAIRY-FREE OPTION: Substitute vegan cheese or nutritional yeast for the Parmesan.

HONEY LEMON GRILLED CHICKEN

DF | NF

New Favorite | SERVES **4**

Around here, it's always grilling season. No matter what the weather is like, my dad and brother are always offering to "throw something on the grill." Nothing can deter them from their quest to grill, once they've set their minds to it. In fact, my brother, Ashton, once decided to grill in a rare Georgia snowstorm. He walked out the door carrying a plate of chicken to throw on the grill, *in his bare feet and with shorts on*. A few minutes later, he ran back inside with barely cooked chicken. "It's cold!" he said by way of excuse. "Put some pants on and get back out there and cook this chicken right," Mom said. When he went back outside, he was wearing shoes. Although you may not want to grill this during a snowstorm, it's a perfect summer meal, thanks to the addition of a new favorite ingredient, ginger.

1 cup honey

⅓ cup freshly squeezed lemon juice

⅓ cup soy sauce

½ teaspoon ground ginger

½ teaspoon freshly ground
    black pepper

1 tablespoon minced garlic

4 boneless, skinless chicken breasts

PREP TIME: 10 minutes, plus 30 minutes marinating time

COOK TIME: 15 minutes

PER SERVING: Calories: 428; Total fat: 2g; Saturated fat: 0g; Cholesterol: 81mg; Carbs: 73g; Fiber: 1g; Protein: 34g; Sodium: 1300mg

1. In a gallon-size freezer bag, combine the honey, lemon juice, soy sauce, ginger, pepper, and garlic.

2. Add the chicken, seal the bag, and toss to coat. Refrigerate to marinate for at least 30 minutes.

3. Preheat a grill to high heat.

4. Remove the chicken from the marinade (throw away the marinade) and place it on the grill over direct heat. Cook for 5 to 6 minutes. Turn the chicken and grill the other side for 5 to 6 minutes more.

MAKE-AHEAD TIP: Chicken needs to marinate for at least 30 minutes for flavor, but it can safely marinate for up to 2 days in the refrigerator.

VARIATION TIP: If it's not grilling season or you don't have a grill, bake the chicken. Preheat the oven to 350°F. Spray a 3-quart casserole dish with nonstick cooking spray and place the marinated chicken in it. Bake for 20 minutes or until the chicken is no longer pink.

GLUTEN-FREE OPTION: Use gluten-free soy sauce or tamari.

CHICKEN AND VEGGIE SKILLET

GF | **NF**

Updated Classic | SERVES **6**

Whenever we travel, we stop in locally owned restaurants and enjoy the local cuisine. If we like a dish, we dissect the ingredients and re-create it at home. My son—a food science major—tells me all the unusual ingredients. With one unusual risotto we had, I couldn't quite decide on the elusive ingredient. He knew right away, "It's saffron, Mom." *Well, I'm glad I paid that college tuition.*

Then there are rare times when the restaurant owners outright give me the recipe. I was at Silver Dollar City in Branson, Missouri, where I had one of their skillet meals. Our group joked that it tasted so good because we'd helped stir the giant skillet. Their PR team heard how much we enjoyed the meal and emailed us a copy of the recipe. I made some changes—adding tomatoes, fresh garlic, and some herbs, and swapping zucchini instead of yellow squash. Now it's just the way I like it. Experiment with your own favorite vegetables. It's a good way to use up those extras from the garden.

4 tablespoons (½ stick) salted butter, plus more as needed

4 or 5 ears fresh corn, shucked, kernels cut from the cob

4 or 5 zucchini, sliced

3 cups fresh okra, sliced

1 medium yellow onion, diced

1 medium green bell pepper, diced

2 tablespoons minced garlic

3 cups diced cooked chicken

2 or 3 medium tomatoes, diced

1 tablespoon Italian seasoning or herbes de Provence

1 teaspoon salt

1 teaspoon freshly ground black pepper

Cooked rice, for serving (optional)

PREP TIME: 30 minutes

COOK TIME: 20 minutes

PER SERVING: Calories: 291; Total fat: 12g; Saturated fat: 6g; Cholesterol: 76mg; Carbs: 24g; Fiber: 6g; Protein: 26g; Sodium: 516mg

1. In a large skillet over medium-high heat, melt the butter.

2. Add the corn, zucchini, okra, onion, bell pepper, and garlic. Sauté for 12 to 15 minutes, until the vegetables are tender, stirring often. Add more butter to the pan, if needed.

3. Stir in the chicken, tomatoes, Italian seasoning, salt, and pepper. Sauté for 2 to 3 minutes more, stirring constantly. Remove from the heat. Serve over cooked rice (if using).

INGREDIENT TIP: If fresh vegetables are not in season or you're in a hurry, substitute an equal amount of frozen or canned vegetables.

DAIRY-FREE OPTION: Substitute ¼ cup vegan butter (we use Earth Balance Soy Free Blend).

BARBECUE SHRIMP *page 117*

Seven

FISH OR CUT BAIT
—
SEAFOOD

BRITTANY Some of my earliest memories involve fish. My Great-Aunt Kay and Great-Uncle Hermit lived on a catfish farm. Some weekends, I would meet my cousins there to play while the adults talked. If we were lucky, Hermit would take some time away from the chatter to take us down to explore the fish farm. Other weekends, Goondaddy would meet up with Dawes, another brother, and we'd go fishing down on the river. A few times a year, we all gathered on the Tennessee River for a family reunion. There were fish there, too. As for eating them, we took a yearly pilgrimage to a catfish restaurant that overlooked the Tennessee River from the side of Raccoon Mountain. I don't remember what the food tasted like, but I'll never forget the view! Weekends were spent at a local church's fish fry with my grandparents and my friends. When I make some of the recipes in this chapter, sometimes with friends during fish fries at the creek, I'm instantly transported back to my childhood. I hope they bring you good memories, too.

OVEN-FRIED CORNMEAL PECAN CATFISH WITH LEMON THYME MAYONNAISE

DF

Updated Classic | SERVES **4**

My Uncle Hermit raised catfish on his farm. His pond, which doesn't seem as large now as when I was a child, seemed to go on forever. Each evening, he took a five-gallon bucket of food to the pond to feed the fish. As soon as the first pellets hit the water, a swarm of catfish appeared—tails and fins flashing—as they greedily gobbled the food. I raced to the edge of the pond and dipped my feet in the water, then pulled them back, shrieking, as the catfish nibbled my toes.

After the food was gone and the last fish had disappeared, we'd stand silently at the pond, gazing out over the woods. The spell wasn't broken until we heard Aunt Kay yelling, "Dinner!" As much as I liked the catfish in the pond, I couldn't turn down my aunt's fried catfish, served with crunchy coleslaw and hushpuppies, crisp and fresh from the fryer. This is the perfect tribute recipe. I've added pecans and made the fish baked instead of fried, but it's still delicious, especially with lemon thyme straight from the garden in this mayonnaise.

FOR THE CATFISH

Nonstick cooking spray

½ cup dry bread crumbs

½ cup cornmeal

1 teaspoon Old Bay seasoning

¼ teaspoon salt

¼ teaspoon cayenne pepper

¼ cup finely chopped pecans, toasted (see how-to tip on page 85)

1 tablespoon cooking oil

4 (4-ounce) catfish fillets

1 large egg, beaten

PREP TIME: 15 minutes

COOK TIME: 6 to 15 minutes, depending on the size of the fillets

FOR THE SAUCE

¼ cup mayonnaise

3 tablespoons freshly squeezed lemon juice

2 tablespoons minced fresh lemon thyme

PER SERVING: Calories: 372; Total fat: 21g; Saturated fat: 4g; Cholesterol: 115mg; Carbs: 26g; Fiber: 2g; Protein: 22g; Sodium: 576mg

TO MAKE THE CATFISH

1. Preheat the oven to 500°F. Coat a baking dish with cooking spray, and set it aside.

2. In a shallow bowl, stir together the bread crumbs, cornmeal, Old Bay seasoning, salt, and cayenne until blended.

3. Mix in the pecans.

4. Add the oil to the pecan–bread crumb mixture. Stir to combine.

5. Brush each catfish fillet lightly with beaten egg. Dip each fillet, one at a time, into the bread crumb mixture to coat on both sides. Place the fillets in the prepared baking dish.

6. Bake, uncovered, for 6 to 8 minutes for each ½ inch of thickness, or until the fish flakes easily with a fork.

TO MAKE THE SAUCE

While the fish is baking, mix the mayonnaise, lemon juice, and fresh lemon thyme until blended. Serve with the catfish.

DID YOU KNOW?: Alabama, Arkansas, Louisiana, and Mississippi produce 94 percent of the farm-grown catfish in the United States.

GLUTEN-FREE OPTION: Use gluten-free bread crumbs.

SHRIMP AND GRITS

NF

Updated Classic | SERVES **4**

During one of our travels, we stayed at a lovely bed and breakfast, the Anchorage 1770, in Beaumont, South Carolina. Each morning, breakfast choices included some of the best, creamiest, richest grits I've ever tasted. We ordered them *every morning* and sent our compliments to the chef and owners. Let's face it, y'all. Grits can be iffy—you never know if you're going to get the unsalted, hard as a rock, flavorless version. No wonder some people say they don't like grits. We did some experimenting to come up with a cheesy version of the Anchorage 1770's grits. I don't know Chef Byron's secret recipe, but I think these grits are a good substitute. Be sure to use traditional, uncooked grits and not the quick cooking variety, which just won't work in this recipe.

FOR THE GRITS

1 cup stone-ground grits
3 tablespoons minced fresh parsley
1 teaspoon salt
1 (8-ounce) package cream cheese, cut into 1-inch cubes, at room temperature
3½ cups boiling water
1 cup heavy (whipping) cream

PREP TIME: 25 minutes

COOK TIME: 1 hour

PER SERVING: Calories: 874; Total fat: 66g; Saturated fat: 34g; Cholesterol: 354mg; Carbs: 26g; Fiber: 3g; Protein: 46g; Sodium: 1826mg

FOR THE SHRIMP

8 bacon slices
1 large yellow onion, diced
1 large bell pepper, any color, diced
1 pound uncooked large shrimp, peeled and cleaned
¼ cup all-purpose flour
2 teaspoons minced garlic
½ teaspoon salt
½ teaspoon cayenne pepper
2 cups chicken broth
1 large tomato, diced
5 drops hot sauce

TO MAKE THE GRITS

1. In a large saucepan over low heat, combine the grits, parsley, and salt.

2. Stir in the cream cheese, boiling water, and cream. Simmer for 1 hour, stirring frequently, until thick and creamy.

TO MAKE THE SHRIMP

1. Once the grits have cooked for about 30 minutes, in a large skillet over medium heat, fry the bacon for 5 minutes or until crispy. Reserve 4 tablespoons of bacon grease. Discard any remaining grease and transfer the bacon to a paper towel–lined plate. Once it is cool enough to handle, crumble the bacon and set it aside.

2. Pour the reserved bacon grease back into the skillet. Place the skillet over medium heat and add the onion and bell pepper. Sauté for 5 to 7 minutes, until tender.

3. Stir in the shrimp. Cook for 2 to 3 minutes, stirring constantly, until the shrimp turn pink.

4. Stir in the flour, garlic, salt, cayenne, and crumbled bacon. Cook for 1 minute, stirring constantly.

5. Add the chicken broth. Reduce the heat to medium-low and cook for 3 minutes, or until thickened, stirring constantly. Remove from the heat.

6. Stir in the tomato and hot sauce.

7. To serve, spread the creamy grits on a serving platter, and top with the shrimp mixture.

VARIATION TIP: You can also cook the grits in a slow cooker. Coat the insert with cooking spray and combine all the grits ingredients in it. Stir. Cover the pot and cook for 4 hours on low heat, stirring occasionally.

GLUTEN-FREE OPTION: Substitute gluten-free all-purpose flour.

"THE REST OF THE COUNTRY HAS LONG WANTED WHAT SOUTHERNERS HAVE. THEY COVET OUR STONE-GROUND GRITS."

—JOHN T. EDGE

SIMPLE POACHED FISH

New Favorite | SERVES **4**

I was a junior in college when I married Bryan. We didn't see each other often because our schedules clashed. On one of the few nights during the week we'd have dinner together, I tried to create a special meal. The fancy meals I wanted to serve were out of our budget, leaving me looking for ways to *doctor* them. One day, I came across a recipe for mock lobster that called for fish fillets instead of lobster. When Bryan asked what we were having for dinner, I told him, "Lobster—sort of." Seeing his slightly terrified look, I encouraged him: "Just try it." He surprised himself by enjoying it. It's become one of my favorite quick and easy ways to cook fish.

¼ cup freshly squeezed lemon juice

2 tablespoons salt

1 small yellow onion, chopped

2 bay leaves

1 quart water

4 (4-ounce) sole or monkfish fillets

1 teaspoon paprika

Melted salted butter, for serving (optional)

Fresh minced parsley, for garnishing (optional)

PREP TIME: 15 minutes

COOK TIME: 30 minutes

PER SERVING: Calories: 137; Total fat: 2g; Saturated fat: 1g; Cholesterol: 75mg; Carbs: 2g; Fiber: 1g; Protein: 26g; Sodium: 698mg

VARIATION TIP: Sometimes I serve it with lime mint sauce instead of the melted butter. Just mix 1 cup plain yogurt with ¼ cup fresh chopped mint, 1 tablespoon lime juice, 1 teaspoon lime zest, ¼ teaspoon salt, and ¼ teaspoon pepper.

1. In a small bowl, stir together the lemon juice, salt, onion, and bay leaves.

2. In a large saucepan over high heat, combine the water and lemon-salt mixture. Bring to a boil. Reduce the heat to maintain a simmer, and simmer for 20 minutes.

3. Add the fish. Simmer for 10 minutes. Remove the fish from the liquid and transfer to a paper towel–lined plate to drain.

4. Sprinkle the fish with the paprika. Serve with melted butter and garnish with parsley (if using).

DID YOU KNOW?: In the Middle Ages, a lemon slice was served with fish because it was believed the acidity would destroy any bones accidentally swallowed.

HOW-TO TIP: If your family doesn't like the taste of frozen fish, thaw it in milk. It will taste fresher!

EASY SHRIMP CREOLE

Heirloom Recipe | SERVES **6**

The first time I visited New Orleans, I was a teenager and ready to *laissez les bon temps rouler* (let the good times roll)! I fell in love with the French Quarter—the quaint shops, Jackson Square, the slow-rolling Mississippi River, and, of course, the food. Why had no one introduced me to Cajun and Creole delicacies before? On each trip to New Orleans, I would speak to the locals and seek out the authentic Cajun and Creole restaurants tucked into side streets. I learned the correct way to eat crawfish, discovered the joys of king cake and boudin balls, and, when feeling touristy, stopped for fresh, hot beignets at Café Du Monde. But one dish always reminds me of my favorite flavors of New Orleans—shrimp Creole. Whenever I want a taste of Louisiana, I whip this up.

4 tablespoons (½ stick) salted butter

1 small yellow onion, chopped

⅓ cup pitted green olives, chopped

2 tablespoons minced garlic

5 medium tomatoes, chopped

1 medium green bell pepper, chopped

1 bay leaf

2 tablespoons chopped fresh parsley

2 teaspoons sugar

½ teaspoon salt

½ teaspoon cayenne pepper

1 teaspoon chopped fresh thyme

2 pounds raw shrimp, peeled, deveined, and cleaned

6 cups cooked rice

PREP TIME: 30 minutes

COOK TIME: 1 hour, 5 minutes

PER SERVING: Calories: 504; Total fat: 12g; Saturated fat: 5g; Cholesterol: 295mg; Carbs: 64g; Fiber: 3g; Protein: 36g; Sodium: 797mg

1. In a large saucepan over low heat, melt the butter.

2. Add the onion, green olives, and garlic. Cover the pan and simmer for 2 minutes.

3. Add the tomatoes, bell pepper, bay leaf, parsley, sugar, salt, cayenne, and thyme. Stir to combine. Simmer the mixture for 50 minutes, stirring occasionally, or until the sauce is thick.

4. Add the shrimp. Cook for 10 minutes, stirring occasionally, until the shrimp is opaque. Serve hot over the cooked rice.

DID YOU KNOW?: Cajuns add flavor to their cooking with what they call the "holy trinity:" onion, bell pepper, and celery.

INGREDIENT TIP: Many old recipes list "fat" as an ingredient. This means use real butter.

FOIL-BAKED FISH WITH PARSLEY-LEMON BUTTER

GF | NF

New Favorite | SERVES **4**

When I was little, Grandmother and Pawpaw would take me with them to Friday night fish frys at a little local country church. They ran through Lent and would sometimes take place in the summer when a congregation member had an especially prolific fishing trip. My favorite part wasn't the food, but rather the fact that my best preschool friend, Jon, was also there. While the adults talked and prepared the food, he and I played hide-and-seek with other members of the church. My grandparents had forgotten the kind of trouble kids can get into, so we weren't particularly well supervised. This was usually no problem, but as we got older, we took more risks finding the perfect hiding spot. This culminated in me locking Jon in the trunk of a car and forgetting him when I was called to eat. *It took his parents a while to find him, and we sure were better supervised after that.* Although this fish is baked instead of the traditional fried, it's the kind of food I abandoned Jon for. This is delicious topped with fresh parsley lemon butter.

FOR THE FISH

4 (4- to 6-ounce) cod or flounder fillets
¼ cup grated Parmesan cheese
1 teaspoon cayenne pepper
1 medium zucchini, sliced
1 medium bell pepper, any color, cut into strips
1 medium yellow onion, cut into strips

FOR THE BUTTER

4 tablespoons (½ stick) salted butter
1 tablespoon freshly squeezed lemon juice
¼ cup chopped fresh parsley

PREP TIME: 20 minutes

COOK TIME: 20 minutes

PER SERVING: Calories: 269; Total fat: 15g; Saturated fat: 8g; Cholesterol: 86mg; Carbs: 7g; Fiber: 2g; Protein: 28g; Sodium: 256mg

TO MAKE THE FISH

1. Preheat the oven to 450°F.

2. Cut four (12-by-18-inch) pieces of aluminum foil. Center 1 fish fillet on each foil sheet.

3. In a small bowl, stir together the Parmesan and cayenne. Sprinkle this mixture over the fish.

4. Top each fish with one-fourth of the zucchini, bell pepper, and onion.

5. Fold the foil over to seal and create packets. Place the packets on a baking sheet.

6. Bake for 18 to 22 minutes or until the vegetables are tender and the fish flakes easily with a fork. Serve hot.

TO MAKE THE BUTTER

Melt the butter in a small saucepan over low heat, and then stir in the lemon juice and parsley. Serve over the fish.

DID YOU KNOW?: Glues made from fish were once used in painting, manuscripts, and adhesives. The earliest recorded use was in ancient Egypt, about 3,500 years ago.

DAIRY-FREE OPTION: Substitute vegan cheese and vegan butter.

VARIATION TIP: If it's grilling season, preheat a grill to high heat. Place the (very well-sealed) foil packets directly on the grill. Grill for 5 to 7 minutes per side or until the fish flakes easily with a fork.

SHRIMP REMOULADE

Heirloom Recipe | SERVES **4**

While Justin and I were engaged, we visited New Orleans with my mom and little brother. I remember two things vividly: the ghost tour, which caused me to have a panic attack when we returned to the hotel (I've never felt more like spirits lurked around every corner than I did in New Orleans that night) and the food. Beignets, jambalaya, po'boys with Louisiana remoulade—all delicious in the New Orleans way that they aren't in any other city. Although I would love to forget some of the terrifying tales I heard on the ghost walk, I never want to forget the food. This remoulade sauce is so good. For the full effect, eat it on a stone patio while surrounded by ivy and revelers. *A strong cocktail wouldn't hurt the ambience, either.*

¼ cup prepared horseradish

1 tablespoon freshly squeezed lemon juice

2 teaspoons spicy brown mustard

3 tablespoons chopped fresh chives

2 tablespoons minced onion

¼ teaspoon salt

¼ teaspoon freshly ground black pepper

2 pounds boiled shrimp, shells removed, chilled

PREP TIME: 15 minutes

PER SERVING: Calories: 281; Total fat: 4g; Saturated fat: 1g; Cholesterol: 346mg; Carbs: 6g; Fiber: 1g; Protein: 52g; Sodium: 809mg

1. In a small bowl, stir together the horseradish, lemon juice, and mustard.

2. Add the chives, onion, salt, and pepper. Stir to combine.

3. Serve the shrimp with the sauce poured over it, or dip the shrimp into the remoulade.

HOW-TO TIP: To make your own prepared horseradish, use 2 cups chopped, peeled fresh horseradish root, ¾ cup white vinegar, and 1 teaspoon salt. Put the horseradish in a blender with 2 tablespoons of vinegar. Process until smooth. Transfer to a pint-size jar and add the salt and remaining 10 tablespoons of vinegar. Stir to combine. Cover and keep refrigerated.

MAKE-AHEAD TIP: The remoulade can be made 24 hours in advance, allowing the flavors to blend to perfection.

BARBECUE SHRIMP

GF | **NF**   *New Favorite* | SERVES **6** TO **8**

When my dad was a little younger than I am now, he, his brother, and his dad went down to Apalachicola for a deep-sea fishing trip. They took a charter boat out into the Gulf of Mexico and fished their little hearts out. After a long, hard day, they returned to shore absolutely starving. They weren't in the mood for fish—unsurprisingly—but they still wanted some of that Gulf seafood. They found a little backwater restaurant where, according to family legend, they had the best shrimp of their lives. The fishing trip has become family lore, and although we have no idea if that restaurant even still exists, they still love some barbecue shrimp. You can make it yourself with this recipe—the twist of coconut rum gives the traditional barbecue shrimp a smooth flavor—and see if it lives up to their hype.

4 pounds large shrimp, unpeeled

1 cup (2 sticks) salted butter or margarine, melted

½ cup barbecue sauce (your favorite)

½ cup coconut rum (see ingredient tip)

¼ cup olive oil

½ teaspoon garlic salt

½ teaspoon celery salt

½ teaspoon Creole seasoning

Juice of 4 lemons

1 tablespoon freshly ground black pepper

PREP TIME: 10 minutes

COOK TIME: 10 minutes

PER SERVING: Calories: 671; Total fat: 39g; Saturated fat: 21g; Cholesterol: 513mg; Carbs: 14g; Fiber: 1g; Protein: 57g; Sodium: 883mg

DAIRY-FREE OPTION: Use vegan butter.

1. Preheat the broiler to its highest setting.

2. Place the unpeeled shrimp in a heavy, oven-safe pan.

3. In a medium bowl, stir together the melted butter, barbecue sauce, rum, olive oil, garlic salt, celery salt, Creole seasoning, and lemon juice, adjusting the seasoning to taste. Pour this over the shrimp. Sprinkle the shrimp with the pepper. Place the pan on the middle rack of the oven and bake for 5 minutes.

4. Remove from the oven and stir.

5. Return the shrimp to the oven. Bake for 5 minutes more, or until the shrimp are cooked through. Serve hot with crusty bread for dipping, if desired.

INGREDIENT TIP: The coconut rum can be replaced with an equal amount of apple juice, white grape juice, or pineapple juice.

CRAB CAKES

Heirloom recipe | SERVES **4**

When Justin and I got married, we honeymooned on the Georgia coast. Although I remember a lot of things about that trip—days spent lazing on the beach, the two days at the water park, and picnicking under the pines—nothing stands out to me more than the food. We visited small, local restaurants that used the best produce and seafood Georgia had to offer. But no restaurant could compete with one particular meal. In Brunswick, we found a seafood market that had fresh fish and seafood every morning. You could buy whole fish to grill or fry, or you could have it prepared at the market. We had it prepared there. We ate huge Georgia shrimp, fresh fish, and my favorite, Georgia blue crab. It was unassuming, served in Styrofoam takeout boxes. They forgot to give us silverware, so we ate with our hands under the hot sun. Whenever I make crab cakes, I think fondly of that wonderful meal.

½ teaspoon dry mustard

½ teaspoon salt

½ teaspoon cayenne pepper or hot sauce

½ teaspoon freshly ground black pepper

2 tablespoons mayonnaise

1 pound fresh crabmeat

¼ cup finely chopped fresh parsley

2 tablespoons grated onion

½ cup seasoned bread crumbs

1 large egg, beaten

2 tablespoons peanut or vegetable oil

1. In a large bowl, stir together the mustard, salt, cayenne, and black pepper.

2. Add the mayonnaise. Stir to combine.

3. Add the crabmeat, parsley, and onion. Stir until the crabmeat is coated.

4. Add the bread crumbs and egg. Stir until combined. Shape the mixture into about 8 (2-inch) patties.

5. In a large skillet over medium-high heat, heat the peanut oil.

PREP TIME: 15 minutes

COOK TIME: 6 minutes per batch

PER SERVING: Calories: 273; Total fat: 13g; Saturated fat: 2g; Cholesterol: 139mg; Carbs: 13g; Fiber: 1g; Protein: 24g; Sodium: 957mg

6. Working in batches, place the crab cakes in the skillet, but do not crowd them. Cook for 2 to 3 minutes, until browned. Flip and continue cooking for 1 minute more. Lower the heat to medium and cook the crab cakes for 2 minutes more. Transfer to paper towel–lined plates to drain, and pat to remove excess oil.

GLUTEN-FREE OPTION: Substitute gluten-free all-purpose flour.

HOW-TO TIP: To keep parsley fresh, fill an 8-ounce jar halfway with water. Place the parsley stems in the water and loosely cover the leaves with a plastic produce bag. Change the water every 2 days.

"THE SOUTH CAME WITH ME WHEREVER I WENT. MY MANNER, MY PALATE, MY ACCENT, MY APPRECIATION OF HUMIDITY."

—ALLISON GLOCK

SCALLOPS IN WINE SAUCE

GF | **NF**

New Favorite | SERVES **6**

After Justin and I were married, he decided to learn to cook. One of his first dishes, Tacos for Hunger, was an unmitigated disaster. Justin invited my family over for dinner to show off his new cooking skills. They walked in and immediately started coughing. Even our dog, who is low to the ground, was coughing. "What are you cooking, Justin?" Mom asked. "It's making my eyes burn!" "I think I added too many hot peppers," he responded. While my mom opened windows, Justin proudly sat his *very small* dish of tacos on the table. Everyone stared at the dish before my mom blurted, "Do we have any sides?" "Oh, no," Justin said, "I thought this was plenty." After eyeing the dish a few minutes, my mom said, "I'm not sure this will feed six people." We praised his efforts and the rest of the family went home and had another meal. Now, he's an excellent cook and can make dishes like these scallops. It's one of our favorites to serve to company. The Parmesan gives the traditional wine sauce added character. For a change of pace, substitute Asiago cheese.

Nonstick cooking spray

1 cup white wine

1½ teaspoons salt

2 pounds scallops

¾ cup salted butter, melted

2 tablespoons chopped fresh parsley

1 teaspoon garlic powder

½ cup grated Parmesan cheese

PREP TIME: 15 minutes

COOK TIME: 20 minutes

PER SERVING: Calories: 402; Total fat: 26g; Saturated fat: 16g; Cholesterol: 118mg; Carbs: 5g; Fiber: 0g; Protein: 29g; Sodium: 967mg

1. Preheat the oven to 450°F. Coat a 2-quart casserole dish with cooking spray, and set it aside.

2. In a large saucepan over medium-high heat, combine the wine and salt. Bring to a boil.

3. Add the scallops. Reduce the heat to a simmer and cook for 3 minutes. Drain the scallops and place them in the prepared casserole dish.

4. In a small bowl, stir together the melted butter, parsley, and garlic powder. Pour this mixture evenly over the scallops.

5. Sprinkle with the Parmesan.

6. Bake for 12 minutes, until the scallops are opaque.

DAIRY-FREE OPTION: Substitute vegan butter and vegan cheese.

HOW-TO TIP: You can substitute dried herbs for fresh. For each tablespoon of fresh herbs in a recipe, use 1 teaspoon of dried herbs.

LEMON GRILLED FISH WITH DILL MAYONNAISE

GF | **NF**

New Favorite | SERVES **6**

The one and only time I went deep-sea fishing was when I was 16. My uncle Jim, brave man that he was, took five of us—all teens—out for "the experience." I'd never been on the ocean before and was thrilled about all the fish I planned to catch. The boat ride out was exhilarating. I could have cruised around the ocean all day. Eventually, we stopped and prepared for fishing. The sea was as calm as a millpond, the sun was shining, and it promised to be the perfect day. I grabbed my rod, threw it into the water, and waited for fish to bite. *That's when I noticed a queasy feeling.* I spent the rest of the trip lying on the top deck of the boat, breathing through my mouth and trying to avoid the fish smells. I decided in the future I would forego fishing trips and stick to buying my fish from the store. This recipe makes me—almost—forget about the seasickness. We give the grilled fish a punch with the creamy fresh dill mayonnaise.

3 tablespoons melted salted butter

3 tablespoons freshly squeezed lemon juice

2 teaspoons garlic powder

¼ teaspoon salt

¼ teaspoon freshly ground black pepper

¼ teaspoon paprika

6 tilapia or sole fillets

½ cup mayonnaise

1 tablespoon spicy brown mustard

2 tablespoons grated Parmesan cheese

2 teaspoons minced onion

½ teaspoon minced fresh dill

PREP TIME: 15 minutes, plus 30 minutes marinating time

COOK TIME: 8 to 15 minutes

PER SERVING: Calories: 234; Total fat: 14g; Saturated fat: 6g; Cholesterol: 77mg; Carbs: 6g; Fiber: 0g; Protein: 22g; Sodium: 361mg

1. In a gallon-size freezer bag, combine the melted butter and lemon juice.

2. Add the garlic powder, salt, pepper, and paprika.

3. Add the fish. Seal the bag and shake gently to coat the fish. Refrigerate to marinate for 30 minutes.

4. Preheat an outdoor grill or a broiler to high heat.

5. In a small bowl, stir together the mayonnaise, mustard, Parmesan, onion, and dill. Keep refrigerated until ready to use.

6. Remove the fish from the marinade and place it on the grill. Close the lid and cook for 8 minutes for each inch of thickness, or until the fish flakes easily with a fork, turning halfway through the cooking time. Alternatively, place the fish on a baking sheet and broil it for 5 minutes for each inch of thickness.

7. Top each fillet with about 1 tablespoon of the dill mayonnaise.

HOW-TO TIP: To store fresh fish in the freezer, tightly wrap each fillet in aluminum foil, and then seal the fish in an airtight freezer bag. Use within 2 to 3 months for fatty fish like salmon, and within 6 to 8 months for lean fish like cod or catfish.

OLD-FASHIONED GLAZED HAM *page 138*

Eight

LIVING HIGH ON THE HOG 'TIL THE COWS COME HOME

PORK AND BEEF

PAM I grew up with a mom who was vegetarian. She would cook meat for my dad and me once or twice a week, but it wasn't everyday fare. Then I met Bryan. He believed meat was a necessary accompaniment for a meal. I'm talking bacon or sausage gravy for breakfast, sandwiches for lunch, and fried pork chops or fried chicken for dinner. *Every. Single. Day.* I like variety in my meals, so I tried preparing many different pork and beef recipes. Some were amazing. Some were flops. Once, when trying a new dish made with leftovers, my dad told me, "Well, this ain't the best thing we ever ate." My son was also quick to tell me if a recipe should not be repeated. *And he started early.* At age 4, he poked a piece of quiche on his plate and said, "I hope this tastes better than it looks." After one bite, he looked at me seriously and said, "Blech! It doesn't!" The recipes in this chapter—even those that began as flops—are ones the entire family agrees are winners.

STUFFED CABBAGE ROLLS

| DF | GF | NF |

Heirloom Recipe | SERVES **8**

When I was newly married, I asked Bryan to share some of his favorite recipes to add to our menu, which included recipes the kids still complain about—like hash brown casserole and hamburger corn casserole. One favorite he mentioned several times was stuffed cabbage rolls. I was confused. Having escaped my mom's mostly vegetarian cooking, which included lots of stewed cabbage, *I couldn't understand why anyone would willingly put meat with their cabbage.* "I'll make it," I said, "but I don't understand why you would ruin good hamburger." Strangely enough, I liked it. What's more, it became one of my son's favorites when he was a preschooler. If I didn't make stuffed cabbage often enough to suit his tastes, he would complain to his Grandmother Wattenbarger that he *needed* stuffed cabbage. She would make a batch for him and send any leftovers home for him to enjoy the next day. That is, if Bryan didn't find them first!

FOR THE STUFFED CABBAGE ROLLS

1 large (about 3-pound) head cabbage, leaves carefully peeled off (you'll need 12 to 16 whole leaves, or more if you like to use 2 leaves per roll)

1 pound lean ground beef

1 cup uncooked rice

1 tablespoon chili powder

4 large tomatoes, chopped

1 large yellow onion, diced

¼ cup chopped fresh parsley

1½ teaspoons salt

½ teaspoon freshly ground black pepper

PREP TIME: 20 minutes

COOK TIME: 1 hour, 20 minutes

FOR THE SAUCE

1¾ cups water

1 (8-ounce) can tomato sauce

½ cup packed light brown sugar

¼ cup freshly squeezed lemon juice

2 tablespoons ketchup

1 bay leaf, crumbled

PER SERVING: Calories: 296; Total fat: 5g; Saturated fat: 2g; Cholesterol: 35mg; Carbs: 50g; Fiber: 7g; Protein: 16g; Sodium: 1567mg

TO MAKE THE STUFFED CABBAGE ROLLS

1. Preheat the oven to 350°F.

2. Bring a large pot of water to a boil over high heat. Add the cabbage leaves and boil for 5 minutes. Transfer the leaves to a colander.

3. In a medium bowl, mix together the ground beef, rice, chili powder, tomatoes, onion, parsley, salt, and pepper until well blended. Place 1 tablespoon of the meat mixture near the stem end of each cabbage leaf. Wrap the leaves in and around the meat. Secure each leaf with a toothpick, if desired, and place the cabbage rolls, seam-side down, in a 3-quart baking dish.

TO MAKE THE SAUCE

1. In a medium bowl, stir together the water, tomato sauce, brown sugar, lemon juice, ketchup, bay leaf, and 1¾ cups of water. Pour the sauce over the cabbage rolls. (An additional teaspoon of salt can be added, if desired.)

2. Cover the dish with aluminum foil and bake for 1 hour, 15 minutes. (Use a knife to cut open one of the rolls, making sure the meat is brown and the rice and cabbage are soft.)

INGREDIENT TIP: If fresh tomatoes are not in season or you are in a hurry, use 1 (28-ounce) can of chopped tomatoes instead of the fresh tomatoes.

"CAULIFLOWER IS NOTHING BUT CABBAGE WITH A COLLEGE EDUCATION."

—MARK TWAIN

COLLARD GREENS WITH HAM

GF | **NF**

Heirloom Recipe | SERVES **8**

Working at the farmers' market gave me a fresh appreciation for turnip and collard greens. The farmers at the booth behind me are the sweetest people I've ever met, and I looked forward to seeing what they brought from their small farm to the market each week. Sometimes it was tiny cherry tomatoes in every color imaginable. And sometimes, it was greens. I've always enjoyed turnip greens, but I've never really cared about them. Greens are greens, right? But seeing how the farmers carefully inspected all the greens and seeing the customers turn them over, looking for any imperfection the farmers may have missed . . . well, that started my quest for the perfect turnip greens. This is it.

2 pounds collard greens or
     turnip greens
1 ham bone or 1½ cups cubed
     cooked ham
1 medium yellow onion, diced
4 tablespoons (½ stick) salted butter
1 to 2 teaspoons salt
1 teaspoon freshly ground
     black pepper
½ teaspoon sugar

PREP TIME: 20 minutes

COOK TIME: 1 hour

PER SERVING: Calories: 136; Total fat: 8g; Saturated fat: 5g; Cholesterol: 30mg; Carbs: 11g; Fiber: 4g; Protein: 6g; Sodium: 708mg

1. Place the collard greens in a sink filled with cold water. Wash each green individually. Drain the water, refill the sink, and wash once more (see how-to tip).

2. Remove and discard the stems from the greens.

3. Put the greens in a large saucepan or Dutch oven and cover with enough water to submerge them.

4. Add the ham bone, onion, butter, salt, pepper, and sugar. Bring the greens to a boil over high heat. Reduce the heat to medium-low and simmer for about 1 hour, stirring occasionally, until the greens are tender. Add more water as needed.

HOW-TO TIP: To choose the perfect collard greens, look for bunches with bright green leaves that are not wilted and have no signs of yellowing or browning. Sometimes it's hard to remove the grit from fresh greens. The grit comes right off if you add salt to the cleaning water.

HAM AND CHEESE OVEN PANCAKE

NF | *New Favorite* | SERVES **4**

I work for a farmer who sells cheese, and I love meeting new people and getting to discuss the recipes they create with our cheese. It's fun to debate which cheese would go perfectly with the tomatoes they're bringing home, and suggest the perfect cheese for a date-night charcuterie board. It's less fun to answer questions like, "Does he milk all the goats, even the males?" for the third time, trying to keep a straight face. If you were at our cheese stand right now, I would suggest a very sharp Cheddar for this oven pancake. This recipe is also super easy to make gluten free (see gluten-free option). *You can thank me later.* Having company? Top the pancake with 1 cup of fresh spinach sautéed with ½ teaspoon of fresh minced garlic in step 6, and substitute Gruyère cheese for the Cheddar.

3 large eggs, beaten

½ cup all-purpose flour

½ cup 2% or whole milk

½ teaspoon salt

1 tablespoon salted butter, melted, plus more for the skillet

1 cup cubed cooked ham

1 medium yellow onion, diced

½ cup shredded sharp Cheddar cheese

PREP TIME: 15 minutes

COOK TIME: 20 minutes

PER SERVING: Calories: 274; Total fat: 15g; Saturated fat: 7g; Cholesterol: 184mg; Carbs: 18g; Fiber: 2g; Protein: 17g; Sodium: 907mg

GLUTEN-FREE OPTION: Substitute gluten-free all-purpose flour.

1. Preheat the oven to 450°F.

2. In a medium bowl, whisk the eggs, flour, milk, salt, and melted butter until blended.

3. Stir in the ham and onion.

4. Grease the bottom and sides of a 12-inch cast iron skillet with butter.

5. Pour the pancake mixture into the skillet and bake for 15 minutes.

6. Remove the pancake from the oven and top with the cheese.

7. Return the pancake to the oven. Reduce the temperature to 350°F and bake for 5 minutes, until puffy and golden brown.

HOW-TO TIP: To tell if eggs are fresh, place them in water. If they sink, they're fresh. If they float, they should not be used.

BACON AND TOMATO PIE

Heirloom Recipe | SERVES **6**

Tomatoes are one of my favorite things about living in the South. I anxiously await tomato season, when the farmers across from my farmers' market booth sell nothing but homegrown tomatoes. At the end of my shift (or before, if the gruff but lovable farmer I work for takes pity on me), I rush across the aisle to purchase tomatoes in every color. My favorites are the Mr. Stripey variety, with their big bands of yellow and light red and their slightly sweet taste. My husband is partial to a good beefsteak, and my daughter will never turn down a handful of "chocolate sprinkles," tiny, dark red grape tomatoes with green stripes. Try making this recipe with your favorite variety of heirloom tomatoes. It tastes best when tomatoes are in season.

4 large tomatoes, peeled and sliced

½ cup chopped scallions

8 to 10 fresh basil leaves, chopped

1 (9-inch) frozen piecrust

1 teaspoon salt

1 teaspoon freshly ground
    black pepper

1 cup shredded mozzarella cheese

1 cup shredded Cheddar cheese

1 cup mayonnaise

5 bacon slices, cooked and crumbled

1. Preheat the oven to 350°F.

2. Layer the tomato slices, scallions, and basil in the piecrust.

3. Sprinkle with the salt and pepper.

4. In a small bowl, stir together the mozzarella, Cheddar, mayonnaise, and crumbled bacon. Pour the cheese mixture over the layered tomatoes, and spread it out evenly.

5. Bake for 30 minutes or until the center is set.

PREP TIME: 15 minutes

COOK TIME: 30 minutes

PER SERVING: Calories: 460; Total fat: 34g; Saturated fat: 10g; Cholesterol: 50mg; Carbs: 26g; Fiber: 2g; Protein: 14g; Sodium: 1131mg

GLUTEN-FREE OPTION: Use a gluten-free piecrust.

HOW-TO TIP: To pick the most flavorful tomatoes at the store, look for tomatoes with no light yellow or green patches. These can be an indicator the tomatoes were picked before they were fully ripe, which means that they will have less flavor than vine-ripened ones.

SOUTHERN STYLE "REFRIED" HAM AND PINTO BEANS

DF | GF | NF

Updated Classic | SERVES **8**

My Pawpaw loved pinto beans. Whenever he ate them, he'd put a little hot sauce in them. Whether it was a normal hot sauce or some pepper vinegar, it didn't really matter to him. What mattered was that your beans should burn your mouth when you ate them—hot off the stove and spiced until your eyes watered. Now, thanks to our Guatemalan friends, we've updated our classic recipe.

1 pound dried pinto beans, picked over for debris, soaked overnight in a large bowl with enough water to cover
2 teaspoons minced garlic
1 teaspoon salt
1 teaspoon chili powder
1 teaspoon ground cumin
1 quart water
1 cup diced cooked ham
1 large yellow onion, diced
2 teaspoons lime juice

PREP TIME: 20 minutes, plus 12 hours soaking time

COOK TIME: 5 hours

PER SERVING: Calories: 238; Total fat: 2g; Saturated fat: 1g; Cholesterol: 10mg; Carbs: 39g; Fiber: 10g; Protein: 15g; Sodium: 523mg

1. Drain the beans and put them in a slow cooker.

2. Sprinkle with the garlic, salt, chili powder, and cumin. Stir to combine, then pour in the water.

3. Cover the slow cooker and cook for 4 hours on low heat.

4. Add the ham and onion. Replace the lid and cook for 1 more hour on low heat.

5. Stir in the lime juice.

6. Mash the beans to your desired consistency before serving.

VARIATION TIP: Alternatively, you can make this on the stove top. Place the soaked beans in a stockpot, cover with 1 inch of water, and add the seasonings as desired. Bring the beans to a boil over high heat. Reduce the heat to a simmer and add the ham and onion. Cover the pot loosely and simmer for 1 hour, stirring occasionally. Continue with the recipe as written.

PORK CHOPS WITH CARAMELIZED ONIONS AND PEPPERS

| DF | GF | NF |

New Favorite | SERVES **4**

My grandmother lived in an older home and didn't believe in all the modern comforts. I was 16 before she purchased her one window air conditioner to cool the entire house. Even then, it wasn't turned on unless the temperature soared over 90 degrees. My mom followed her lead. The kitchen was sweltering when we cooked. One day, while working in the kitchen preparing this recipe, Brittany, who was two, sat on the window seat watching a chicken below. She pushed her arms against the screen, trying to get a better view. Well, the screen popped out and she fell out of the window on top of the chicken. *There was much screaming and squawking*. We rushed to check on her. Thank goodness it was a short fall—she *and the chicken* were unharmed. Whenever I make these pork chops, I remember the confused look on that poor chicken's face. Balsamic vinegar gives this dish its new Southern taste, and I know my grandmother would approve.

3 tablespoons olive oil

1 teaspoon garlic salt

4 boneless pork chops

1 large red bell pepper, seeded, cut into strips

1 medium yellow onion, diced

2 teaspoons minced garlic

2 teaspoons sugar

1 tablespoon balsamic vinegar

PREP TIME: 10 minutes

COOK TIME: 15 minutes

PER SERVING: Calories: 291; Total fat: 20g; Saturated fat: 5g; Cholesterol: 50mg; Carbs: 9g; Fiber: 1g; Protein: 20g; Sodium: 43mg

1. In a large skillet over medium-high heat, heat the olive oil.

2. Sprinkle the garlic salt evenly over the pork chops. Place the pork chops in the skillet. Cook for 6 minutes, turning occasionally, until the chops are evenly browned on both sides. Transfer the pork chops to a serving platter. Cover with aluminum foil to keep warm.

3. Place the bell pepper, onion, garlic, and sugar in the skillet and return it to medium heat. Cook for 2 to 3 minutes, stirring constantly, until the onion is light brown.

4. Stir in the vinegar. Cook, stirring, for 1 minute more. Pour the onion and pepper mixture over the chops. Serve over rice, if desired.

HOW-TO TIP: To prevent tears when chopping onions, put them in the freezer for 10 minutes before cutting.

DID YOU KNOW?: Hernando de Soto is known as the father of the American pork industry because he brought pigs to present-day Tampa Bay, Florida, from Spain in 1539.

BREADED PORK CHOPS WITH AVOCADO-PEACH SALSA

NF

New Favorite | SERVES **4**

My husband, Justin, works as a Spanish interpreter at a local hospital. Through his work, we've become involved in the local Latino community, with which we share a need for hospitality, a love of fried chicken, and a desire for warm weather. They've shared some of their favorite recipes with us, like carne asada, tamales, and chicken soup, *although I leave out the chicken feet.* We've returned the favor with some of our favorites, like this basic breaded pork chop recipe, pepped up with fresh spices and a peach-avocado salsa. Our friends serve theirs with black beans, while we prefer pintos. We all agree this should be eaten in the presence of loved ones, with a tall glass of sweet tea to wash it down.

FOR THE PORK CHOPS

1 cup fresh bread crumbs

½ cup shredded Parmesan cheese

1 tablespoon minced fresh parsley, or 1 teaspoon dried

1 tablespoon minced fresh oregano, or 1 teaspoon dried

1 tablespoon minced fresh basil, or 1 teaspoon dried

2 large eggs, beaten

4 pork chops (about 2 pounds)

2 tablespoons olive oil

FOR THE SALSA

1 avocado, diced

1 peach, peeled and diced

1 tablespoon lime juice

½ teaspoon salt

¼ cup fresh cilantro leaves, chopped (optional)

PREP TIME: 15 minutes

COOK TIME: 6 minutes

PER SERVING: Calories: 596; Total fat: 27g; Saturated fat: 7g; Cholesterol: 209mg; Carbs: 29g; Fiber: 7g; Protein: 60g; Sodium: 1022mg

TO MAKE THE PORK CHOPS

1. In a shallow bowl, stir together the bread crumbs, Parmesan, parsley, oregano, and basil. Pour the beaten eggs into another shallow bowl.

2. Dip the pork chops first into the egg mixture and then into the bread crumb mixture to coat on both sides.

3. In a medium skillet over medium heat, heat the olive oil.

4. Place the pork chops in the hot skillet. Cook for 3 minutes. Flip the pork chops and cook for 2 to 3 minutes more, until a meat thermometer registers 145°F. Remove from the heat and let the pork chops rest for 3 minutes before serving.

TO MAKE THE SALSA

1. While the pork chops rest, combine the avocado, peach, lime juice, salt, and cilantro (if using) in a medium bowl. Stir until just combined.

2. Plate the pork chops and top with the salsa.

VARIATION TIP: Preheat the oven to 425°F. Coat a 3-quart casserole dish with nonstick cooking spray and place the pork chops in it. Drizzle them with olive oil and sprinkle with the spices and cheese. Bake for 10 minutes, turn, and bake for 10 minutes more.

DAIRY-FREE OPTION: Use vegan Parmesan cheese.

GLUTEN-FREE OPTION: Use gluten-free bread crumbs.

"WE SOUTHERNERS ARE PICKY ABOUT OUR INGREDIENTS. ALMOST SNOOTY. WE'LL DRIVE OUT OF THE WAY TO GET TO A FARM STAND WHERE WE KNOW THE PEACHES ARE RIPE AND THE TOMATOES ARE STILL WARM FROM THE FIELD."

—DAVID DIBERNEDETTO

GARLIC AND ROSEMARY PORK TENDERLOIN

DF | GF | NF

New Favorite | SERVES **8**

Raising kids on a farm has advantages. There's plenty of room to run and play, and friendly animals quickly become pets. Mine is an original Southdown Babydoll sheep named Nikolai. *I know, weird name.* Whenever a visitor sees Nikolai, they exclaim, "Looks like good eating!" My family, however, knows Nikolai is with us until he dies from old age. This brings us to our failed adventure raising our own pork, which we call "The Pig Fiasco."

Bryan decided we should raise a pig: "Think of the money we'll save on pork!" So we did. Bryan named him Freezer—so the kids would remember his destiny and wouldn't become attached. As the day approached for Freezer to be slaughtered, the kids said they would refuse to eat the meat. Well, Bryan and I ate a lot of poor Freezer by ourselves, as the kids were good to their word. We purchase all our meat from the grocery store now, and we sure do love this tenderloin—seasoned with fresh rosemary picked right from our garden.

1 cup white vinegar

1 cup honey

½ cup minced fresh rosemary

2 tablespoons minced garlic

1½ teaspoons salt

½ teaspoon freshly ground
   black pepper

1 (3-pound) boneless pork tenderloin

PREP TIME: 10 minutes, plus 30 minutes to 2 hours marinating time

COOK TIME: 1 hour

PER SERVING: Calories: 331; Total fat: 5g; Saturated fat: 2g; Cholesterol: 90mg; Carbs: 40g; Fiber: 2g; Protein: 32g; Sodium: 773mg

1. Preheat the oven to 325°F.

2. In a medium bowl, whisk the vinegar, honey, rosemary, garlic, salt, and pepper. Divide the mixture into two equal amounts; place half in a small bowl in the refrigerator, and spoon the other half into a gallon-size freezer bag.

3. Add the pork tenderloin to the freezer bag. Seal the bag and shake to coat. Refrigerate the tenderloin to marinate for at least 30 minutes and up to 2 hours.

4. Remove the tenderloin from the marinade and place it in a 2-quart baking dish. Discard the marinade. Add the reserved marinade to the dish and cover it with aluminum foil.

5. Bake for 1 hour or until a meat thermometer shows an internal temperature of 145°F. Let the pork rest for 3 minutes before serving.

INGREDIENT TIP: Not a fan of rosemary? Replace it with an equal amount of fresh chives, basil, savory, dill, or fennel.

VARIATION TIP: You can make this in a slow cooker. Prepare as directed, but cook the pork tenderloin in a slow cooker, covered, for 3½ hours on high heat or 5 hours on low heat.

OLD-FASHIONED GLAZED HAM

GF | **NF**

Heirloom Recipe | SERVES **15** TO **20**

During the holidays, everyone helps prepare the meal. It's *usually* a fun, festive occasion. But one Easter, the ham was baking, the pies were wrapped, and sweet smells drifted from the stove top. The day was perfect—until I heard Brittany announce, "Mom, the oven is on fire!" I was quick to respond: "Is it a big fire or a small fire?" Brittany (with a look of mild amazement) said, "It's a medium fire and getting bigger." Because Brittany had a history of making bad situations in the kitchen worse, I told her, "Close the door and DO NOT pour water on the elements." Bryan immediately took charge, extinguishing the fire with baking soda and smothering it with a towel. I pulled the ham from the oven, and we gazed at it sadly. "I think we could wipe off the ashes," Ashton said, grabbing the paper towels. Minutes later he pronounced it "good as new." Justin, who had missed the excitement, strolled in and grabbed a piece of ham. "This is delicious," he declared. It stayed our secret—the perfect holiday meal, *even if you have to remove the ashes.*

1¼ cups water

1 (15-ounce) can crushed pineapple

1 (10-ounce) bottle maraschino cherries, drained with the juice reserved

½ cup white vinegar

1 cup packed light brown sugar

2 tablespoons ground cloves

2 tablespoons cornstarch

2 tablespoons salted butter

1 (8- to 10-pound) frozen cooked spiral ham, thawed

PREP TIME: 15 minutes

COOK TIME: 50 minutes

PER SERVING: Calories: 492; Total fat: 26g; Saturated fat: 7g; Cholesterol: 124mg; Carbs: 36g; Fiber: 1g; Protein: 34g; Sodium: 1654mg

1. Preheat the oven to 350°F.

2. In a medium saucepan over medium heat, combine the water, crushed pineapple, reserved cherry juice, and vinegar.

3. Stir in the brown sugar, cloves, cornstarch, and butter. Cook for 3 to 5 minutes, stirring constantly, until the mixture thickens. Remove from the heat and stir in the cherries.

4. Place the ham in a roasting pan. Spoon the cherry mixture over the ham.

5. Bake for 45 minutes. Use a meat thermometer to make sure that the meat has reached an internal temperature of 140°F.

INGREDIENT TIP: Uncooked ham can be substituted for the cooked spiral ham. Cook the thawed ham at 350°F for 18 minutes per pound.

DAIRY-FREE OPTION: Use vegan butter.

DID YOU KNOW?: The word ham was first used around the fifteenth century to refer to the pork cut from the hind leg of a pig.

ONE BAD DAY

My mom enjoys exploring Kentucky, especially the area around Harrodsburg and Georgetown. We've visited the Shaker Village of Pleasant Hill, located outside Harrodsburg, for the past three years. Each year, we've found different activities. Last year, we took a tour called "First Flavors: A Spring Farm Tasting," which wound around the farm area. We'd stop at different garden plots, discuss Shaker history and farming methods, and then taste some of the produce, picked fresh from the vine.

After touring the garden plots, we visited some of the farm animals. When we stopped at the pig stall, our guide explained how their restaurant, The Trustees' Table, believed in the farm-to-table movement. "We use as much fresh produce grown in our gardens as we can," she said. "And we raise our own meat."

My mom, who has a soft spot for animals she raises, asked, "Don't you get attached to the pigs? We raise sheep and everyone knows my sheep are pets. They'll wander around the farm, fat and happy, until they die of old age." "Well," our guide replied, seriously, "I like to think of it like this: These pigs live a good life with one bad day."

My mom's stunned look was priceless. We finished our tour and had lunch at their farm-to-table restaurant. I had the barbecue pork, and it was delicious.

—*Ashton Wattenbarger*
(PAM'S SON AND BRITTANY'S BROTHER)

SLOW-COOKED BARBECUE PORK

DF | GF | NF

Updated Classic | SERVES **8**

We served barbecue at my wedding. It was a barn wedding, which is trendy now, but this was different. For one, it was a working barn. We spent the day of the rehearsal shoveling hay out of the hayloft. I'm allergic to straw, so my eyes were puffy and red. *It was anything but glamorous.*

On the day of the wedding, we danced to Brad Paisley and served barbecue out of disposable aluminum pans. We almost passed out from the heat. It was perfect. Whenever I eat barbecue, I reminisce.

Our recipe makes a tart barbecue sauce instead of the sweeter version. You have to use spicy brown mustard—regular mustard will not do. If you like a saucier pork, make a double batch of sauce and serve half on the side with the cooked pork.

1 (3-pound) pork roast

1 large yellow onion, diced

2 teaspoons minced garlic

½ cup ketchup

½ cup packed light brown sugar

½ cup water

¼ cup white vinegar

1 tablespoon prepared spicy brown mustard

½ teaspoon salt

½ teaspoon freshly ground black pepper

1. Place the pork roast in a slow cooker. Add the onion and garlic.

2. In a small bowl, stir together the ketchup, brown sugar, water, vinegar, mustard, salt, and pepper. Pour the sauce over the roast. Cover the slow cooker and cook for 4 hours on high heat or 8 hours on low heat.

3. Remove the pork roast from the slow cooker and shred the meat with two forks. Serve.

PREP TIME: 15 minutes

COOK TIME: 4 to 8 hours

PER SERVING: Calories: 259; Total fat: 7g; Saturated fat: 2g; Cholesterol: 98mg; Carbs: 15g; Fiber: 1g; Protein: 32g; Sodium: 728mg

VARIATION TIP: For a twist, add ¼ cup of bourbon and ¼ cup of molasses to the sauce.

HOW-TO TIP: To choose the freshest pork, look for meat that doesn't have discolored spots or a grayish-pink color.

INGREDIENT TIP: You can substitute a beef roast (3 to 4 hours on high or 6 to 8 hours on low) or chicken legs (5 to 8 hours on low, or until the juices run clear and the meat is no longer pink on the inside) for the pork roast in this recipe.

HAMBURGER RICE CASSEROLE

GF | NF

Updated Classic | SERVES **6**

When I don't feel like cooking, we either have "hallelujah night" or a dish I throw together at the last minute. Bryan coined the term "hallelujah night" once, when the kids asked what we were having for dinner. "We're having leftovers," I said. "It's hallelujah night," Bryan said. "You'll eat whatever you can find in the fridge and say, 'Hallelujah, we have dinner.'"

When my son, Ashton, a food science major, is home from college, we'll dig around the refrigerator to find ingredients that sound good together. Our latest creation was an adaption of my mom's hamburger casserole recipe to make it gluten free. *We christened it "Pot o' Beef."* In honor of my mom, we gave it a fancier name for this book, but whatever you call it, you'll say "hallelujah!"

1 pound lean ground beef

3 celery stalks, diced

1 large yellow onion, diced

1 large bell pepper, any color, diced

4 or 5 large tomatoes, diced, or
   1 (16-ounce) can diced tomatoes

2 cups cooked rice

1 cup tomato sauce

1 tablespoon Worcestershire sauce

½ teaspoon salt

½ teaspoon freshly ground
   black pepper

½ teaspoon dried oregano

½ cup grated Cheddar cheese

PREP TIME: 15 minutes

COOK TIME: 40 minutes

PER SERVING: Calories: 278; Total fat: 9g;
Saturated fat: 4g; Cholesterol: 57mg; Carbs: 29g;
Fiber: 3g; Protein: 21g; Sodium: 565mg

1. Preheat the oven to 350°F.

2. In a large oven-safe skillet over medium heat, combine the ground beef, celery, onion, and bell pepper. Cook for about 10 minutes, breaking up the beef with the back of a spoon, until browned. Drain the beef and transfer it to a large bowl.

3. Add the tomatoes, rice, tomato sauce, Worcestershire sauce, salt, pepper, and oregano to the beef. Stir to combine. Transfer the mixture to the skillet.

4. Sprinkle with the cheese.

5. Put the skillet in the oven and bake for 30 minutes, or until the meat is no longer pink and the rice is soft. Remove the skillet from the oven and let it sit for 10 minutes before serving. This allows time for the juices to absorb, making it easier to slice.

INGREDIENT TIP: Replace the rice with 2 cups cooked gluten-free or regular egg noodles.

STUFFED ZUCCHINI

GF | **NF**

Updated Classic | SERVES **5**

This recipe is perfect for those times when you accidentally leave your car unlocked during church and someone sneaks a bag of zucchini on your backseat. If that seems like a bizarre and outlandish scenario, well, it's a true story. We attended a small rural congregation at the time, so the idea of someone breaking into the car barely even occurred to Mom. However, when she left church, her car had been disturbed. What had been taken? Absolutely nothing. Instead, a paper sack filled to the brim with zucchini had been deposited on the backseat. There were many suspects, and the culprit was never apprehended. *Since then, Mom always locks the car before heading into church.* This recipe is an adaptation of a traditional stuffed pepper recipe.

Nonstick cooking spray

5 medium zucchini, ends trimmed

1 pound lean ground beef

1 large yellow onion, chopped

1 cup sliced mushrooms

1 tablespoon garlic powder

¼ teaspoon salt

¼ teaspoon freshly ground
    black pepper

8 ounces cream cheese, cubed

PREP TIME: 20 minutes

COOK TIME: 50 minutes

PER SERVING: Calories: 340; Total fat: 23g;
Saturated fat: 12g; Cholesterol: 106mg; Carbs: 12g;
Fiber: 3g; Protein: 24g; Sodium: 341mg

1. Preheat the oven to 350°F. Coat a 9-by-13-inch baking dish with cooking spray, and set it aside.

2. Place the zucchini in a large saucepan and cover them with water. Bring the water to a boil over medium-high heat. Reduce the heat to medium-low and cook the zucchini for 10 minutes. Remove the zucchini from the water and set them aside to cool.

3. Halve the cooled zucchini lengthwise. Scoop out the insides, leaving a ½-inch-thick shell. Dice the scooped-out zucchini flesh.

4. In a medium skillet over medium heat, cook the ground beef for about 10 minutes, breaking it up with the back of a spoon, until browned. Drain the grease and return the skillet with the beef to medium heat.

5. Stir in the onion, mushrooms, diced zucchini flesh, garlic powder, salt, and pepper. Cook for about 5 minutes, stirring often, until the onion is tender.

6. Drain the beef mixture again, if needed, and stir in the cream cheese until it melts.

7. Place the zucchini shells in the prepared baking dish. Spoon equal amounts of the meat mixture into each shell.

8. Bake for 25 minutes, until everything is heated through.

DID YOU KNOW?: Zucchini was first cultivated in Central and South America and later introduced in Europe. The word *zucchini* comes from the Italian *la zucchina*, meaning "small squash."

DAIRY-FREE OPTION: Use vegan cream cheese.

GREEN PEPPER STEAK

DF | GF | NF

Heirloom Recipe | SERVES **4**

Whenever my dad goes to a local restaurant, he gets steak. Not a traditional steak, mind you. Nope. He gets either a hamburger steak, chicken fried steak, or pepper steak. It's been this way for years. He barely even has to look at a menu if it's Southern food they're offering. He knows what he wants, and he never wavers. He and my brother have a ranking of the restaurants around us. They determine which has the best pepper steak, the best sweet tea, and the best fries. I wouldn't be surprised if they have these things written down with a serious commentary about the logic behind their choices. Unfortunately for my dad and brother, they can't go out to eat every night. On those nights, they're lucky we have a great recipe for making pepper steak at home—and this gluten-free version means everyone can enjoy it.

¼ cup vegetable oil

1 pound round steak, cut into 1-inch strips

3 celery stalks, diced

1 large green bell pepper, cut into strips

1 teaspoon ground cloves

1 teaspoon gluten-free soy sauce (tamari)

1 teaspoon salt

1¼ cups water, divided

1 tablespoon cornstarch

2 cups cooked rice

PREP TIME: 20 minutes

COOK TIME: 30 minutes

PER SERVING: Calories: 450; Total fat: 22g; Saturated fat: 4g; Cholesterol: 69mg; Carbs: 32g; Fiber: 1g; Protein: 28g; Sodium: 643mg

INGREDIENT TIP: Cornstarch is added as a thickening agent. If you don't have cornstarch, substitute an equal amount of flour.

1. In a medium skillet over medium heat, heat the vegetable oil.

2. Add the steak. Cook for about 5 minutes, until browned.

3. Add the celery, bell pepper, cloves, tamari, salt, and ¼ cup of water. Simmer for 15 to 20 minutes, stirring occasionally, or until the vegetables and meat are tender.

4. In a small bowl, stir together the cornstarch and remaining 1 cup of water. Slowly stir this cornstarch mixture into the beef mixture. Cook for about 5 minutes, stirring constantly, until the mixture thickens. Serve the pepper steak over the cooked rice.

HOW-TO TIP: To make fresh poultry, beef, or pork easier to slice, just pop it in the freezer for 5 to 10 minutes, until it is just barely frozen.

HAMBURGER PIE

New Favorite | SERVES **8**

Casseroles are the backbone of the South, made and given away for any occasion. When one of my friends was recently diagnosed with terminal cancer, my first thought was, *I need to make her a casserole.* I'm not sure how a casserole would help, other than to relieve some of the burden of cooking, but it seemed the appropriate choice for the situation.

While I thought casseroles were recent inventions, they date back to medieval times. The first recipe for a casserole was written by a member of the court of King Charles II of Anjou. That's a recipe from somewhere between 1254 and 1309! This hamburger pie is an adaptation of a classic beef casserole. Serving it in a piecrust makes it perfect for little hands. Sometimes, we substitute veggie "meat" crumbles to accommodate our vegan friends.

1 pound lean ground beef

1 medium bell pepper, any color, chopped

1 medium yellow onion, chopped

1 large egg, beaten

⅓ cup ketchup

1 teaspoon chili powder

1 frozen piecrust, baked

¾ cup shredded mozzarella cheese

PREP TIME: 15 minutes

COOK TIME: 30 minutes

PER SERVING: Calories: 201; Total fat: 11g; Saturated fat: 3g; Cholesterol: 61mg; Carbs: 13g; Fiber: 1g; Protein: 14g; Sodium: 290mg

DAIRY-FREE OPTION: Substitute vegan cheese.

GLUTEN-FREE OPTION: Use a gluten-free piecrust.

1. Preheat the oven to 350°F.

2. In a medium skillet over medium heat, combine the ground beef, bell pepper, and onion. Cook for about 10 minutes, breaking up the meat with the back of a spoon, until browned. Drain off the grease and transfer the meat mixture to a medium bowl.

3. Add the egg, ketchup, and chili powder to the meat. Mix until blended. Spoon the meat mixture into the piecrust.

4. Bake for 12 minutes.

5. Sprinkle the cheese on top and bake for 3 to 5 minutes more, or until the cheese is melted.

HOW-TO TIP: To choose the freshest bell peppers, look for those with green stems and no wrinkles, sunken places, or black spots.

CHICKEN FRIED STEAK WITH GRAVY

NF

Heirloom Recipe | SERVES **4**

I think it was my dad who once told me, "If you can eat it, you can fry it." This is the unofficial Southern motto, and nowhere more evident than our local festivals and fairs. One of our favorite local festivals is the Corn Bread Festival, held in South Pittsburg, Tennessee, every April. If you're in the know, you'll slip away from the crowds for lunch and head a couple of streets over to the Dixie Freeze, a tiny restaurant that's been around for as long as anyone can remember. You'll order a milkshake and a chicken fried steak for a great price, then lean back and people watch. If you can't make it to the Corn Bread Festival, you'll have to make do with this recipe. To get the full experience, leave your curtains open and gossip about passers-by while you eat.

FOR THE CHICKEN FRIED STEAK

⅔ cup all-purpose flour
¼ teaspoon salt
¼ teaspoon freshly ground
　　black pepper
2 large eggs, beaten
4 cube steaks
¼ cup vegetable oil

FOR THE GRAVY

½ cup all-purpose flour
½ teaspoon salt
½ teaspoon freshly ground
　　black pepper
3 cups whole milk

PREP TIME: 15 minutes

COOK TIME: 25 minutes

PER SERVING: Calories: 693; Total fat: 35g; Saturated fat: 9g; Cholesterol: 248mg; Carbs: 33g; Fiber: 1g; Protein: 59g; Sodium: 601mg

TO MAKE THE CHICKEN FRIED STEAK

1. In a shallow bowl, combine the flour, salt, and pepper. Place the beaten eggs in another shallow bowl.

2. One at a time, dip the steaks first into the flour mixture and then into the egg mixture.

3. Dip the steaks into the flour mixture once more.

4. In a large skillet over medium-high heat, heat the vegetable oil.

5. Add the steaks to the skillet. Cook for 4 to 5 minutes. Turn and cook the other side for 4 to 5 minutes. Transfer the steaks to paper towel–lined plates to drain, leaving the oil in the skillet. Cover the steaks with aluminum foil to keep warm. Return the skillet to medium heat.

TO MAKE THE GRAVY

1. In a small bowl, stir together the flour, salt, and pepper. Add the flour mixture to the reserved cooking oil in the skillet. Stir until blended. Cook the mixture for 3 to 5 minutes, until browned.

2. Slowly stir in the milk. Cook for 5 to 10 minutes, stirring constantly, until the gravy thickens. Serve the gravy over the steak.

DID YOU KNOW?: President William Howard Taft kept a pet cow named Pauline Wayne at the White House.

GLUTEN-FREE OPTION: Substitute gluten-free all-purpose flour.

"EVERY SINGLE DIET I EVER FELL OFF OF WAS BECAUSE OF POTATOES AND GRAVY OF SOME SORT."

—DOLLY PARTON

CLASSIC BAKED BANANA PUDDING *page 162*

Nine

GIVE ME SOME SUGAR
—
DESSERTS

PAM | I admit it. I love sweets. Candy, cookies, cakes, pastries—you name it, I like it. It was hard to decide on these recipes because I had so many to share. And, like all Southern recipes, each one has a memory. "Oh, my mom's chocolate pie! Everyone wanted that recipe." "Here's the recipe for peanut butter cookies Mom used to make for Brittany whenever she spent the night. She NEVER did that for me growing up."

My memories of holidays or extended family get-togethers include the fun times, but also the desserts. All of my aunts and cousins had a specialty dessert. I'd await their arrival, ready to swoop down and help with any last-minute dessert preparation.

As an adult, I'm happy to continue the tradition of making special holiday desserts. Bryan and the kids don't think it's a proper Christmas Eve or Thanksgiving without a caramel pie or brownie trifle. But with our food allergies, we've had to give some of our traditional recipes a new-fangled twist or lighten them up for the rest of the year. It's the South, y'all. We think almost anything can be cured by a good dessert.

CHOCOLATE PIE WITH COCONUT CRUST

GF | V

New Favorite | SERVES **8**

Every family has a "secret family recipe." You know, the one so good everyone wants it. Our family's is my mom's chocolate pie. The smell was enough to pull me away from whatever I might be doing, to investigate. Someone needed to lick the beaters or the spoon, and I was happy to volunteer. I'm still down with licking the spoon and beaters, but my kids have taken over the job from me. For years, too, I thought of this as "funeral pie," because my mom made these whenever she had to take a dish to the funeral home. I didn't want anything bad to happen to anyone, but I *really* liked this pie.

The twist on the traditional recipe—to combine the heirloom filling and meringue recipes with a coconut crust—came from my friend and neighbor, Denise, who has celiac. She swore the combination tasted "just like a Mounds bar." She was right.

FOR THE CRUST

1½ cups shredded coconut

4 tablespoons (½ stick) salted butter or margarine, melted

FOR THE FILLING

¾ cup sugar

3 tablespoons cornstarch

2 tablespoons cocoa powder

¼ teaspoon salt

2 cups whole or 2% milk

3 large egg yolks

1 tablespoon salted butter

1 teaspoon vanilla extract

PREP TIME: 15 minutes

COOK TIME: 35 minutes

FOR THE MERINGUE

3 large egg whites

3 tablespoons sugar

1 teaspoon vanilla extract

PER SERVING: Calories: 328; Total fat: 18g; Saturated fat: 14g; Cholesterol: 94mg; Carbs: 40g; Fiber: 2g; Protein: 6g; Sodium: 225mg

TO MAKE THE CRUST

1. Preheat the oven to 350°F.

2. In a food processor fitted with a standard blade, combine the coconut and melted butter. Process for 30 seconds. Scrape this mixture into an 8-inch pie pan. Pat the crust so it covers the sides and bottom of the pan evenly.

3. Bake for about 15 minutes or until the crust is lightly browned. Leave the oven on.

TO MAKE THE FILLING

1. While the crust bakes, in a medium bowl, stir together the sugar, cornstarch, cocoa powder, and salt.

2. Add the milk and stir to combine. Place the mixture in the top of a double boiler set over medium heat (see how-to tip). Cook for about 5 minutes, stirring constantly, until the mixture is heated through.

3. Transfer ¼ cup of the chocolate mixture to a small bowl. Add the egg yolks and butter. Whisk to combine. Return this mixture to the double boiler. Continue to cook over medium heat for about 8 minutes, stirring constantly, until the mixture thickens. Remove from the heat and stir in the vanilla. Pour the filling into the coconut crust.

TO MAKE THE MERINGUE

1. In a large bowl, use a handheld electric mixer to beat the egg whites, sugar, and vanilla until stiff peaks form. Spread the meringue over the chocolate filling.

2. Bake the assembled pie in the preheated oven for 5 minutes, or until the meringue is lightly browned.

HOW-TO TIP: No double boiler? No worries. You can accomplish the same thing by taking a larger pot, filling it with a few inches of water, and putting a smaller saucepan or heat-resistant bowl on top. The water in the pot should not touch the bottom of the saucepan or bowl. The point of a double boiler is to heat the mixture gently without scorching it.

NUT-FREE OPTION: Coconut is both a fruit and a tree nut. If you have a tree nut allergy, you may prefer to use a gluten-free or regular frozen piecrust instead of the coconut crust. If using a frozen piecrust, prebake the crust for 10 to 12 minutes according to the package directions, or until lightly browned.

PEANUT BUTTER SHEET CAKE

V

Heirloom Recipe | SERVES **16**

When I was little, I loved visiting my goonparents, and I *loved* my Goonmomma's cooking. I don't know what she did, but she could make cheese toast taste like manna from heaven. I would eat anything she cooked. My favorite of her recipes was peanut butter cake. I asked for it almost every time I visited, which was several times a week. Bless her heart—she almost always obliged. Once, she got up at 2 a.m. to make peanut butter cake with me because I had a craving! Whenever I eat this peanut butter cake, I think of her.

FOR THE CAKE

Nonstick cooking spray

2 cups sugar

2 cups all-purpose flour

1 teaspoon baking soda

1 cup (2 sticks) salted butter or margarine, melted

2 large eggs, beaten

1 cup water

½ cup buttermilk

4 teaspoons cocoa powder

1 teaspoon vanilla extract

FOR THE ICING

8 tablespoons (1 stick) salted butter, at room temperature

½ cup peanut butter, crunchy or smooth

1 (16-ounce) box confectioners' sugar

3 to 6 tablespoons heavy (whipping) cream or whole milk

PREP TIME: 30 minutes

COOK TIME: 25 minutes

PER SERVING: Calories: 459; Total fat: 23g; Saturated fat: 13g; Cholesterol: 73mg; Carbs: 61g; Fiber: 1g; Protein: 5g; Sodium: 257mg

TO MAKE THE CAKE

1. Preheat the oven to 350°F. Coat a 9-by-13-inch baking pan with cooking spray, and set it aside.

2. In a medium bowl, stir together the sugar, flour, and baking soda until blended. Set aside.

3. In a large bowl, combine the melted butter, eggs, water, buttermilk, cocoa powder, and vanilla. Using a handheld electric mixer, beat on medium speed until blended.

4. Slowly add the flour mixture to the egg mixture, beating well after each addition. Pour the batter into the prepared pan.

5. Bake for 25 minutes or until a knife inserted into the center comes out clean. Let cool before icing.

TO MAKE THE ICING

1. In a large bowl, combine the butter and peanut butter. Using a handheld electric mixer on medium speed, beat until smooth.

2. Gradually add the confectioners' sugar, mixing well after each addition.

3. Slowly add the cream or milk, 1 tablespoon at a time, mixing after each addition, until the icing reaches your desired consistency—if you like it thicker, use less cream; if you like it thinner, use more. Spread the icing over the cooled cake.

DID YOU KNOW?: The fear of peanut butter sticking to the roof of your mouth is actually a thing! It's called arachibutyrophobia.

INGREDIENT TIP: Sometimes, old recipes call for "one box of 10x sugar." This is equal to one 16-ounce package of confectioners' sugar.

"THIS IS A PLACE WHERE GRANDMOTHERS HOLD BABIES ON THEIR LAPS UNDER THE STARS AND WHISPER IN THEIR EARS THAT THE LIGHTS IN THE SKY ARE HOLES IN THE FLOOR OF HEAVEN."

—RICK BRAGG

FRESH APPLE CAKE

Heirloom Recipe | SERVES **12**

When Bryan and I became engaged, his Grandmother Reeves began inviting me to the weekly Sunday family dinner. I was thrilled, because it meant we'd have at least one of her mouthwatering homemade desserts. I used to swear my mother-in-law, Mary Frances, and Grandmother Reeves always had a dessert handy. Once, at an impromptu family dinner, Mary Frances said, "Oh! I have a coconut cake in the freezer. I'll just pull that out for dessert." *See, I was right.*

I don't like cold or cool weather, but every year, I couldn't wait for fall, when apples were harvested and Grandmother Reeves would make her fresh apple cake. She passed the recipe on to me, and it's still a favorite. It's so versatile. You can use any type of baking apples you prefer.

FOR THE CAKE

Nonstick cooking spray

3 cups all-purpose flour, plus more for
    dusting the cake pan

2 cups sugar

½ cup vegetable oil (see ingredient tip)

3 large eggs

1 teaspoon baking soda

1 teaspoon salt

1 teaspoon vanilla extract

3 cups finely chopped peeled apples
    (see ingredient tip)

1 cup chopped pecans

FOR THE TOPPING

1 cup packed light brown sugar

8 tablespoons (1 stick) salted butter

¼ cup whole milk

PREP TIME: 20 minutes

COOK TIME: 1 hour

PER SERVING: Calories: 486; Total fat: 20g;
Saturated fat: 7g; Cholesterol: 67mg; Carbs: 73g;
Fiber: 2g; Protein: 5g; Sodium: 367mg

TO MAKE THE CAKE

1. Preheat the oven to 350°F. Coat an 8-cup Bundt or tube pan with cooking spray and dust it with flour, knocking out the excess. Set aside.

2. In a large bowl, stir together the flour, sugar, vegetable oil, eggs, baking soda, salt, and vanilla until blended.

3. Fold in the apples and pecans. Pour the batter into the prepared pan.

4. Bake for 1 hour or until a knife inserted into the center comes out clean. Let it cool before removing the cake from the pan.

TO MAKE THE TOPPING

1. While the cake cools, in a small saucepan over medium-high heat, combine the brown sugar, butter, and milk. Bring the mixture to a boil and cook for 3 minutes, stirring constantly.

2. Remove the pan from the heat and let the topping cool. Pour the cooled topping over the cooled cake, and serve.

INGREDIENT TIP: If you prefer, substitute coconut oil for the vegetable oil.

One large apple makes about 1½ cups of finely chopped apples, while 1 medium apple makes about 1 cup of finely chopped apples.

DAIRY-FREE OPTION: Substitute vegan butter, and substitute almond or soy milk for the cow's milk.

GLUTEN-FREE OPTION: Substitute 1-to-1 gluten-free baking flour or gluten-free baking mix for the all-purpose flour.

PECAN PIE TARTS

V | *New Favorite* | MAKES **1** DOZEN

Our family has eaten a lot of pecan pies. Sometimes, my Grandmother Wattenbarger got creative and tried new flavors, like butterscotch pecan pie. Sometimes, my aunt forgot the pie, left it in the oven too long, and burnt the crust. Once, when her dad was sick, it was my mom's turn to make the pecan pie. She bought a frozen one instead of making it herself and transferred it to a nice pie plate. The fact that I remember all these transgressions shows how important the humble pecan pie is to my family, which is why I've never made one myself. Any mistake or flaw would be harshly judged and remembered for 50 years. Instead, I make these pecan pie tarts. They have all the flavors of a traditional pecan pie, but they're a little bit easier to make and a lot less likely to get me ostracized at Christmas.

FOR THE CRUST

Nonstick cooking spray

1 (8-ounce) package cream cheese, at
     room temperature

8 tablespoons (1 stick) salted butter, at
     room temperature

2 cups all-purpose flour, sifted

PREP TIME: 15 to 20 minutes

COOK TIME: 20 minutes

PER SERVING: Calories: 310; Total fat: 19g;
Saturated fat: 6g; Cholesterol: 58mg; Carbs: 33g;
Fiber: 2g; Protein: 4g; Sodium: 80g

FOR THE FILLING

1 cup brown sugar

¼ cup sugar

2 tablespoons salted butter, melted

2 large eggs

1½ tablespoons all-purpose flour

1 tablespoon milk

1 teaspoon vanilla extract

1½ cups chopped pecans

TO MAKE THE CRUST

1. Preheat the oven to 350°F. Coat a 12-cup muffin tin with cooking spray, and set it aside.

2. In a medium bowl, use a handheld electric mixer to cream the cream cheese and butter until blended.

3. Add the flour and mix until completely blended.

4. On a lightly floured surface, roll out the dough to a ½-inch thickness. Using a 2-inch biscuit cutter or glass, cut out 12 dough circles. Re-roll the scraps and cut out more circles, if needed. Place the dough circles in the cups of the prepared muffin tin; press them down so they conform to the cup shape. Set aside.

TO MAKE THE FILLING

1. In a medium bowl, use a handheld electric mixer to mix together the brown sugar, white sugar, butter, and eggs.

2. Add the flour, milk, and vanilla. Stir until blended.

3. Stir in the pecans. Divide the batter evenly among the muffin cups.

4. Bake for about 20 minutes or until the centers are firm but still moist and a knife inserted into the center comes out clean.

HOW-TO TIP: To prolong their shelf life, store pecans in a sealed airtight container in a cool, dry place, such as the refrigerator or freezer.

VARIATION TIP: If you want to stray from the traditional, add ¾ cup mini milk chocolate chips to the batter. A little chocolate never hurt anything.

DAIRY-FREE OPTION: Use vegan butter and vegan cream cheese.

GLUTEN-FREE OPTION: Use gluten-free all-purpose flour.

BUTTERMILK PIE

NF | V

Heirloom recipe | SERVES **8**

I hadn't had buttermilk pie for years until Bryan and I went to our local meat and three restaurant for lunch. The daily special includes a meat and three, a dessert, and a drink for $10.

Bryan and I chose buttermilk pie. "This is the best pie ever," Bryan said as he savored a bite. "I have plenty of buttermilk," I replied. "I can make you one." I dusted off my recipe and made the pie. Then I made an extra because I had a spare piecrust that looked lonely sitting on the counter. I gave away pieces to friends, relatives, and neighbors to sample. Their response was the same: "You have to put this recipe in your book." The pie sounds strange, and people balk at the name, but the end results are delicious.

2 cups sugar

8 tablespoons (1 stick) salted butter, at room temperature

3 tablespoons all-purpose flour

3 large eggs, beaten

1 cup buttermilk

1 teaspoon vanilla extract

1 (9-inch) deep-dish piecrust, unbaked

PREP TIME: 15 minutes

COOK TIME: 50 minutes

PER SERVING: Calories: 422; Total fat: 19g; Saturated fat: 9g; Cholesterol: 102mg; Carbs: 62g; Fiber: 0g; Protein: 5g; Sodium: 243mg

VARIATION TIP: For an updated version, add 3 tablespoons cocoa powder, ½ cup toasted chopped pecans, and a tablespoon of Amaretto.

GLUTEN-FREE OPTION: Use a gluten-free pie shell and substitute gluten-free 1-to-1 baking flour.

1. Preheat the oven to 350°F.

2. In a medium bowl, use a handheld electric mixer to cream the sugar and butter until blended.

3. Add the flour and eggs. Continue to mix until blended.

4. Add the buttermilk and vanilla. Mix well. Pour the mixture into the piecrust. Cover the pie with aluminum foil. (This prevents the edges of the crust from burning.)

5. Bake for 45 to 50 minutes or until a knife inserted into the center of the pie comes out clean. Cool before serving.

INGREDIENT TIP: Have leftover buttermilk? Substitute it for milk in muffins, adding ½ teaspoon baking soda to the recipe for each cup of buttermilk used. Baking soda neutralizes acidity and helps your baked goods rise.

IN THE KITCHEN WITH MARY VEAZEY

My next-door neighbor and dessert test taster, Mary, shared this delicious brownie recipe and story with us.

—*Pam*

The year was 1959. I was newly married and my husband was a broke college student. I took a job at American Life, an insurance company in Atlanta, to help make ends meet. Every Friday, one of our elderly agents, Mr. Bourgerion, drove into town from his home in Alabama. He would arrive at our office with a plate of homemade brownies his wife had made. They were delicious! I asked if she would share the recipe with me. He brought me the recipe the next week. I've been making these for my family ever since.

Mrs. Bourgerion's Brownies

Makes 12

Nonstick cooking spray
½ cup sifted all-purpose flour, plus more for dusting the baking pan
4 tablespoons (½ stick) salted butter, melted

1 cup sugar
2 large eggs
½ cup cocoa powder
1 teaspoon vanilla extract
½ cup walnuts

1. Preheat the oven to 350°F. Coat an 8-by-8-inch baking pan with cooking spray and dust it with flour, knocking out the excess. Set aside.

2. In a large bowl, use a handheld electric mixer to cream the melted butter and sugar until blended.

3. Add the eggs. Mix until blended.

4. Stir in the flour and cocoa powder until blended.

5. Add the vanilla. Stir to combine.

6. Fold in the walnuts. Pour the batter into the prepared pan.

7. Bake for 15 to 20 minutes, until the edges are firm but the center is still moist.

PER SERVING (1 [2-INCH-SQUARE] BROWNIE): Calories: 116; Total fat: 6g; Saturated fat: 3g; Cholesterol: 31mg; Carbs: 15g; Fiber: 1g; Protein: 2g; Sodium: 30mg

SWEET POTATO PIE WITH PECAN TOPPING

V

New Favorite | SERVES **8**

My brother goes to college in Mississippi, where they have a sweet potato festival, which my parents and brother attended one day. Mom came home with a 20-pound bag of sweet potatoes. When Dad asked what we planned to use them for, Mom cryptically replied, "We'll make do." We had sweet potatoes in every form—baked sweet potatoes, sweet potato soup, mashed sweet potatoes, and more—for a few weeks as we raced against time before they rotted. Of all the ways to use them, though, my favorite has to be this updated version of sweet potato pie. The addition of the pecan topping is what makes it really special. It's easy enough to make for a potluck, but fancy enough to serve at your family's Thanksgiving.

FOR THE PIE

2 large sweet potatoes, peeled
    and cooked

1⅓ cups sugar

4 tablespoons (½ stick) salted butter,
    at room temperature

2 large eggs, beaten

½ cup milk

1 teaspoon vanilla extract

½ teaspoon salt

1 (10-inch) piecrust, unbaked

FOR THE TOPPING

1½ cups chopped pecans, toasted
    (see how-to tip on page 85)

1 cup packed light brown sugar

8 tablespoons (1 stick) salted
    butter, melted

PREP TIME: 20 minutes

COOK TIME: 50 minutes

PER SERVING: Calories: 522; Total fat: 28g; Saturated fat: 13g; Cholesterol: 94mg; Carbs: 67g; Fiber: 2g; Protein: 4g; Sodium: 420mg

TO MAKE THE PIE

1. Preheat the oven to 350°F.

2. In a medium bowl, mash the sweet potatoes.

3. Add the sugar and butter. Using a handheld electric mixer, mix until well blended.

4. Add the eggs, milk, vanilla, and salt. Stir well. Pour the mixture into the pie-crust. Set aside.

TO MAKE THE TOPPING

1. In a small bowl, combine the pecans, brown sugar, and melted butter. Stir until combined. Sprinkle the pecan mixture evenly across the top of the pie. Cover the pie with aluminum foil. (This prevents the edges of the crust from burning.)

2. Bake for 45 to 50 minutes or until a knife inserted into the center comes out clean.

INGREDIENT TIP: Old recipes sometimes call for a "dash" of an ingredient. That translates to about ⅛ teaspoon.

DAIRY-FREE OPTION: Use vegan butter and vegan milk.

GLUTEN-FREE OPTION: Use a gluten-free piecrust.

"MY FOUR FAVORITE SOUTHERN FOOD GROUPS ARE BOURBON, SALT, BACON, AND PIE."

—MORGAN MURPHY

CLASSIC BAKED BANANA PUDDING

NF | **V**

Heirloom Recipe | SERVES **12**

Banana pudding is the classic Southern dessert. Every family has their own recipe, and you'll have at least one at every potluck or family dinner. When I got married, I carefully copied our "secret" family recipe.

As newlyweds with different schedules, we didn't see each other often. Bryan, wanting to spend as much time together as possible, helped with meal preparation. One day, while I was making this pudding, he offered to help. "Sure," I said, forgetting he knew absolutely nothing about cooking. I set out two bowls and asked, "Could you separate these eggs for me, please?" "Okay," he said—which, in retrospect, should have been my clue he didn't know what he was doing. "Done," he announced a minute later. I looked up from the pot I was stirring and found the eggs neatly separated—*the eggs in one bowl and shells in another*. I still laugh about that whenever I make this pudding.

FOR THE PUDDING

¾ cup sugar

5 teaspoons all-purpose flour

¼ to ½ teaspoon salt

5 large egg yolks, at room temperature (see ingredient tip)

2½ cups whole or 2% milk

1 teaspoon vanilla extract

1 (11-ounce) package vanilla wafers

5 large bananas, sliced

FOR THE MERINGUE

5 large egg whites, at room temperature (see ingredient tip)

½ cup sugar

½ teaspoon vanilla extract

PREP TIME: 20 minutes

COOK TIME: 20 minutes

PER SERVING: Calories: 304; Total fat: 7g; Saturated fat: 2g; Cholesterol: 95mg; Carbs: 57g; Fiber: 2g; Protein: 6g; Sodium: 185mg

TO MAKE THE PUDDING

1. In a double boiler over medium heat, combine the sugar, flour, and salt. (See how-to tip, page 151, if you don't have a double boiler.)

2. Stir in the egg yolks and milk. Cook for about 10 minutes, stirring constantly, or until the mixture is thick. Remove from the heat and stir in the vanilla.

3. Place the vanilla wafers on the bottom of a 3-quart baking dish, making sure the bottom is covered.

4. Pour the pudding on top of the wafers.

5. Place the sliced bananas on top.

TO MAKE THE MERINGUE

1. Preheat the oven to 350°F.

2. In a medium bowl, using a handheld electric mixer, beat the egg whites, sugar, and vanilla until stiff peaks form. This can take from 5 to 15 minutes.

3. Spread the meringue over the pudding. Bake for 5 to 10 minutes or until the meringue is lightly browned.

INGREDIENT TIP: Let the eggs sit at room temperature for 30 minutes before using, and they'll be easier to whip.

Have leftover bananas? Peel them, break them in half, and freeze in freezer bags. They're great for smoothies or to use in banana bread or muffins.

GLUTEN-FREE OPTION: Use gluten-free all-purpose flour and gluten-free vanilla wafers.

CLASSIC TEA CAKES

NF | **V**

Heirloom Recipe | MAKES **4** DOZEN

When we told our family we were writing a cookbook, my cousins said, "You have to include Aunt Kay's tea cake recipe!" Aunt Kay was the quintessential Southern cook. No matter when a family member visited, you'd find her in the kitchen, an apron tied around her waist. Anything she cooked tasted good, and she always had a sweet treat on hand. We would sneak away from the watchful eyes of our moms to pilfer her peanut brittle or one of these delicious tea cakes. My kids said her recipes were "made with love"—*and a good amount of butter.* This recipe was lost for many years, but I finally found a handwritten copy buried in the bottom of a recipe box. The instructions included vague measurements like "add enough flour to make a firm dough." It was no hardship for my kids to keep mixing batches of these cookies until they had the perfect recipe. If you prefer margarine or butter to shortening, you can substitute, but the cookies will spread.

1 cup packed light brown sugar

1 cup granulated sugar

1 cup vegetable shortening

4 large eggs, beaten

½ cup buttermilk

2 teaspoons vanilla extract

3½ cups all-purpose flour

1 teaspoon baking soda

2 teaspoons baking powder

PREP TIME: 15 to 20 minutes

COOK TIME: 10 to 12 minutes per batch

PER SERVING (1 COOKIE): Calories: 112; Total fat: 5g; Saturated fat: 2g; Cholesterol: 16mg; Carbs: 16g; Fiber: 0g; Protein: 2g; Sodium: 38mg

1. Preheat the oven to 300°F.

2. In a medium bowl, use a handheld electric mixer to cream the brown sugar, granulated sugar, and shortening until fluffy.

3. Add the beaten eggs and buttermilk. Mix until blended.

4. Stir in the vanilla.

5. In a small bowl, stir together the flour, baking soda, and baking powder. Blend the flour into the sugar mixture, ½ cup at a time, mixing just until blended.

6. On a piece of wax paper, roll out the dough to a ¼-inch thickness. Using a 2-inch biscuit cutter or glass, cut out dough circles. Place the tea cakes on a baking sheet. Re-roll the scraps and continue to cut tea cakes.

7. Bake for 10 to 12 minutes or until the tea cakes are lightly browned. Transfer to a wire rack to cool.

INGREDIENT TIP: If the recipe calls for a "pinch" of an ingredient, use about 1/16 teaspoon, or as much as you can pinch between your thumb and forefinger.

VARIATION TIP: Want to update this recipe? Add 1 tablespoon lemon zest to the mixture and drizzle the cooled cookies with melted white chocolate.

GLUTEN-FREE OPTION: Substitute gluten-free 1-to-1 baking flour.

SLOW COOKER APPLE COBBLER

V

Updated Classic | SERVES **8**

Cobbler is as Southern as not owning a pair of snow boots. In fact, it was one of the first things I learned to cook. My best friend, Taylor, and I had picked some wild blackberries in her backyard, and we were determined to turn them into something tasty. Nanny, Taylor's grandmother, patiently walked us through the steps of making our very own cobbler. As it turns out, none of us actually enjoy the taste of wild blackberries, so we never made another wild blackberry dessert. We did learn, however, that we loved cobbler, so it became a regular feature at the dinner table and one of the few things we knew how to cook. This slow cooker version is perfect for potlucks or busy families, because it can be made ahead of time and kept warm. It's also perfect when it's too hot to cook. I like to use this homemade granola topping, but you can use your favorite granola, and I use honey instead of granulated sugar.

FOR THE HOMEMADE GRANOLA

4 cups old-fashioned rolled oats

1 cup finely chopped nuts (walnuts, pecans, almonds, or a mix)

¾ cup honey

½ cup packed light brown sugar

½ cup canola oil

1 teaspoon ground cinnamon

¾ teaspoon salt

1 teaspoon vanilla extract

1 cup semisweet chocolate chips (optional)

1 cup marshmallows (optional)

1 cup dried fruit (optional)

1 cup sweetened or unsweetened coconut flakes (optional)

FOR THE COBBLER

4 medium Granny Smith apples, peeled and sliced

2 cups homemade granola

¼ cup honey

2½ tablespoons salted butter, melted

1 teaspoon ground cinnamon

PER SERVING: Calories: 218; Total fat: 9g; Saturated fat: 3g; Cholesterol: 8mg; Carbs: 37g; Fiber: 3g; Protein: 1g; Sodium: 92mg

PREP TIME: 15 minutes

COOK TIME: 2 hours, 55 minutes

TO MAKE THE HOMEMADE GRANOLA

1. Preheat the oven to 350°F. Line a baking sheet with parchment paper, and set it aside.

2. In a large bowl, combine the oats and nuts.

3. In a saucepan over medium heat, combine the honey, brown sugar, canola oil, cinnamon, and salt. Cook, stirring, until the sugar dissolves. Remove from the heat.

4. Stir the vanilla into the honey mixture. Add the honey mixture to the oats and nuts. Mix well. Spread the granola in an even layer on the prepared baking sheet.

5. Bake for 20 to 25 minutes, stirring occasionally, until crisp and browned. Let cool completely before adding the chocolate chips, marshmallows, dried fruit, or coconut (if using). Refrigerate the granola in an airtight container for up to 1 week.

TO MAKE THE COBBLER

1. Place the sliced apples in a slow cooker.

2. In a medium bowl, stir together the granola, honey, melted butter, and cinnamon. Spread the granola mixture over the apples.

3. Bake for 2½ hours on high heat.

DID YOU KNOW?: Legend says that if you take a bite from an apple and place it under your pillow on Halloween, you will dream of your true love.

DAIRY-FREE AND VEGAN OPTION: Use vegan butter.

GLUTEN-FREE OPTION: Use gluten-free granola.

HEAVENLY APPLE COBBLER

When I was 10, we attended my Great-Uncle Henry's retirement banquet at a local restaurant. Several extended family members drove up from Griffin, Georgia, to attend. I took one bite of the food, and it tasted awful. I glanced around the room; no no one looked as if they were enjoying the meal. As I picked at my plate, trying to think of meals I had enjoyed, I remembered Aunt Oneida's apple cobbler. She had prepared it the last time we visited, and I loved it. *This must be what the angels eat. I've never tasted anything so good*, I thought.

I leaned over to Aunt Oneida and asked her if she would make me a cobbler the next time we visited—and she did! She made an apple cobbler just for me. But she didn't *just* make apple cobbler, she created the entire meal with dishes that complemented the cobbler. And on every visit we made to Griffin in the future, as long as she was alive, she made me an apple cobbler. After she died, the cobbler recipe was lost, but I'd love to be able to taste it one more time.

—*Bryan Wattenbarger*
(PAM'S HUSBAND, BRITTANY'S DAD)

SAND TARTS

V

New Favorite | MAKES ABOUT **2** DOZEN

There's a pecan tree in my Grandmother and Pawpaw's yard. It's lasted through droughts and tornados, and every year it drops hundreds—maybe thousands—of pecans across the grass. Up until my Pawpaw just couldn't, you'd find him under that tree a few times a year, picking up the pecans it had spilled onto the ground. He gathered them into metal buckets, where they sat until Grandmother deigned to crack and toast them and turn them into candies and sweets. They fascinated me, so sometimes Pawpaw would crack a few open for me and let me eat them. They made my tongue feel fuzzy, and I didn't love the woody taste. I was much happier to wait for Grandmother to turn her attention to them and turn them into tasty treats like these sand tarts.

1 cup (2 sticks) salted butter, at room temperature

½ cup confectioners' sugar, plus more for sprinkling

1 teaspoon vanilla extract

1¾ cups all-purpose flour

1 cup chopped pecans

PREP TIME: 15 to 20 minutes

COOK TIME: 30 minutes

PER SERVING (1 COOKIE): Calories: 120; Total fat: 9g; Saturated fat: 5g; Cholesterol: 20mg; Carbs: 10g; Fiber: 0g; Protein: 1g; Sodium: 55mg

1. Preheat the oven to 275°F.

2. In a medium bowl, use a handheld electric mixer to cream the butter and confectioners' sugar until blended.

3. Mix in the vanilla.

4. A little at a time, slowly blend in the flour, then add the pecans. Stir with a wooden spoon, just until the nuts are incorporated.

5. Shape the dough into 1-inch balls and place them on a baking sheet. Press the cookies down with a fork.

6. Bake for 30 minutes. Remove the cookies from the oven and immediately sprinkle confectioners' sugar over top. Transfer to a wire rack to cool.

INGREDIENT TIP: Butter can be frozen for up to 1 year if it is tightly wrapped in aluminum foil and stored in an airtight freezer bag.

VARIATION TIP: If you want to shake things up, substitute toasted almonds or walnuts for the pecans and add ¾ cup white chocolate chips.

DAIRY-FREE AND VEGAN OPTION: Use vegan butter.

GLUTEN-FREE OPTION: Substitute gluten-free 1-to-1 baking flour. (I use Bob's Red Mill.)

STRAWBERRY LEMONADE ICED TEA *page 172*

Ten

DRY AS A BONE

—

DRINKS AND COCKTAILS

BRITTANY It gets hot here in the South—hot, humid, and sticky. You feel like it can't get any hotter, and then it does. That's why a cool, refreshing drink is so important to us. We have mental lists of which restaurants have the best sweet tea, and every county fair has the longest line at the fresh-squeezed lemonade stand. There's a punch for every occasion, from baby shower punch to wedding punch to Christmas punch. I can't remember a holiday or special occasion that didn't have at least five drinks to choose from. However, these recipes aren't just for special occasions. We have sweet teas that are just dandy for porch sitting, which is the official pastime of the Southern summer. These recipes will bring you back to a simpler time, when all you had to worry about was if there'd be enough lemonade to go around after y'all were done hauling hay for the day. They're also fancy enough to serve at your next fancy dinner party—no matter what the season.

STRAWBERRY LEMONADE ICED TEA

DF | GF | NF | V

New Favorite | SERVES **10**

My Pawpaw and Grandmother used to take my cousin and me to the Corn Bread Festival every year. About a 45-minute drive from where we lived, this festival was just what it sounds like—a big fair dedicated to all things corn bread. Although corn bread was the star of the show, *and we ate a lot of it*, we loved the fresh-squeezed lemonade stands that popped up throughout the festival. The lines were long, but it was always worth the wait for that perfect glass of strawberry lemonade. The strawberries were muddled at the bottom of the glass and always clogged up the straw a little. This grown-up version adds another of my favorite drinks, a classic sweet tea, to the mix. With this recipe in hand, you don't have to wait until the next fair to get yourself some.

8 cups water (4 cups cold), divided
2 tea bags
1½ cups sliced fresh strawberries
1¼ cups sugar
1 cup freshly squeezed lemon juice
1 lemon, cut into slices (optional)

PREP TIME: 15 minutes

COOK TIME: 5 minutes

PER SERVING: Calories: 108; Total fat: 0g; Saturated fat: 0g; Cholesterol: 0mg; Carbs: 27g; Fiber: 1g; Protein: 0g; Sodium: 5mg

INGREDIENT TIP: Add different fruits to suit your taste. Try peaches, pineapple, or blueberries instead of strawberries, or use a mix of fruit.

1. In a medium saucepan over high heat, bring 4 cups of water to a boil. Remove from the heat. Add the tea bags and let them steep for 3 to 5 minutes. Remove and discard the tea bags and let the tea cool.

2. In a blender, combine the strawberries, sugar, and lemon juice. Process for 5 to 10 seconds, until blended. Transfer to a medium bowl and add the remaining 4 cups of cold water, stirring until blended.

3. When the tea is cool, stir in the strawberry mixture. Serve over ice, and garnish with lemon slices (if using).

HOW-TO TIP: To keep lemonade from becoming watered down, make a double batch and freeze half in ice-cube trays. Store the frozen lemonade cubes in airtight freezer bags and use them instead of regular ice cubes in your lemonade.

PINEAPPLE-ORANGE MIMOSAS

DF | **GF** | **NF** | **V**   *New Favorite* | SERVES **6**

My great-aunt and great-uncle, Inez and Jim, live in Florida. Their yard always seemed magical to me because it was full of citrus trees. We would pick fresh citrus from the tree and have hand-squeezed orange juice for every meal. Once, when I was a teenager, Jim decided to make harvesting oranges a little easier. We went outside and he asked me to hold a box. Thinking he was going to put oranges in the box as he picked, I stood under the orange tree like he asked. Well, Jim started beating the tree with a rake, causing grapefruit-size oranges to rain down on me like hail. While I stood frozen with shock, Jim started to yell at me to catch the falling fruit in the box. I definitely deserved one of these mimosas after that.

1 (750-milliliter) bottle of
    champagne, chilled
1½ cups freshly squeezed orange
    juice, chilled
¾ cup pineapple juice, chilled
6 tablespoons grenadine (optional)

PREP TIME: 5 minutes

PER SERVING: Calories: 140; Total fat: 0g; Saturated fat: 0g; Cholesterol: 0mg; Carbs: 12g; Fiber: 0g; Protein: 1g; Sodium: 1mg

1. In each of 6 glasses, combine ½ cup of champagne, ¼ cup of orange juice, and 2 tablespoons of pineapple juice. Stir gently with a spoon.

2. Top each with 1 tablespoon of grenadine (if using).

HOW-TO TIP: You can fancy up your mimosa by rimming the glass. Spread sugar or salt evenly over a piece of wax paper, and fill a shallow bowl with water. Dip the rim of the glass in the water, then press it into the sugar or salt. Let dry for 2 to 3 minutes before using.

VARIATION TIP: To make a nonalcoholic version, substitute sparkling white grape juice or lemon-lime soda for the champagne.

LEMON ICE

Heirloom | SERVES **8**

When I was a child, the slushie man visited our neighborhoods during summer. I was allowed one slushie a week—on Fridays—and I made the most of it. I spent all week deciding which flavor I would get, but ended up choosing this lemon ice. By the time my kids came along, the slushie man still drove by my parent's house, and my kids were treated to slushies whenever they visited. We, on the other hand, had an ice cream truck. One day, when the ice cream man came by, this exchange followed:

Kids: "We'd each like an ice cream bar, please."

Ice Cream Man: "That'll be $10."

Me: (*incredulous*) "What? I could buy two boxes of premium ice cream bars for that at the store!"

Much grumbling ensued. Lesson learned—I dug out this gem of a lemon ice recipe. If you prefer, try it with peaches or grapefruit instead.

4½ cups water

2 cups sugar

Zest of 5 medium lemons

Juice of 5 medium lemons, squeezed
    lemons reserved

PREP TIME: 15 minutes, plus 4 to 6 hours chilling time

COOK TIME: 35 minutes

PER SERVING: Calories: 195; Total fat: 0g; Saturated fat: 0g; Cholesterol: 0mg; Carbs: 51g; Fiber: 0g; Protein: 0g; Sodium: 6mg

INGREDIENT TIP: To get more juice from your lemon, submerge the whole fruit in hot water for 15 minutes before juicing.

1. In a medium saucepan over medium-high heat, combine the water and sugar. Cook for 5 minutes, stirring constantly. Remove the pan from the heat.

2. Add the lemon zest, lemon juice, and reserved lemons. Return the lemon mixture to low heat. Simmer for 30 minutes. Strain the mixture and let it cool.

3. Pour the mixture into an airtight freezer container. Freeze for 4 to 6 hours or until frozen. Remove from the freezer 10 to 15 minutes before serving.

HOW-TO TIP: Simple syrup is used in many drink recipes and iced tea. Use 1 part sugar to 1 part water. For example, 1 cup sugar and 1 cup water. Bring the mixture to a boil, stirring constantly, and cook for 3 minutes. Keep the syrup refrigerated.

PEACHY SLUSH COOLER

DF | **GF** | **NF** | **V**

New Favorite | SERVES **4**

I rarely drink, because I don't like the taste of alcohol. So, when I am traveling with friends or for work as a travel writer, I spend quite a bit of time politely sampling the signature drinks and, after a few sips, asking for a Coke. My friends are always surprised when I find a drink I actually like, but they quickly figured out my quirky taste. It has to be light, fruity, and have a low alcohol content. I'll never forget the surprised look on one friend's face when we stopped on a culinary tour and tasted the signature drink. I don't know if it was because I was hot and thirsty or it just tasted so good, but I gulped down the entire drink in seconds. "Did you just drink the *entire thing*?" she asked in amazement. "Yes," I said, "and I'm going to try to re-create it at home." I began experimenting, and this is the result.

2 large peaches, peeled and sliced

1 (6-ounce) can frozen lemonade concentrate

½ cup vodka

2 tablespoons cherry syrup (such as Torani brand)

1 to 2 cups crushed ice, depending on how slushy you like your drink

1. In a blender, combine the peaches, lemonade, vodka, and syrup. Blend for 10 to 12 seconds.

2. Add the ice and blend until the desired consistency is reached.

3. Pour into glasses and serve immediately.

PREP TIME: 10 minutes

PER SERVING: Calories: 187; Total fat: 0g; Saturated fat: 0g; Cholesterol: 0mg; Carbs: 31g; Fiber: 1g; Protein: 1g; Sodium: 2mg

VARIATION TIP: To make a nonalcoholic version, use lemon-lime soda instead of vodka.

To make slushy drinks that won't get watered down as the ice melts, freeze the sliced peaches before adding them to the blender. This way, you won't need to add as much ice.

UPDATED ARNOLD PALMER

| DF | GF | NF | V |

New Favorite | SERVES **6**

Moonshine has come a long way since my relatives in Alabama used to make it in their barn, back when my Goondaddy would make trips to Sand Mountain to pick some up for his famous cough syrup. In fact, moonshine is in vogue now and comes in every flavor you can imagine. I recently tried a jalapeño-flavored moonshine that burned my mouth both from the heat and the alcohol. With moonshine in the spotlight *for reasons besides causing accidental blindness*, it just makes sense that everyone who is anyone is including it in their cocktails. I am no exception. I've had a lot of fun experimenting with different flavors of moonshine and adding them to my favorite drinks. This grown-up Arnold Palmer is one of my favorites.

1 quart water

2 regular tea bags

1 (6-ounce) can frozen lemonade concentrate

½ cup lemon drop moonshine, or to taste

PREP TIME: 5 minutes

COOK TIME: 5 minutes

PER SERVING: Calories: 94; Total fat: 0g; Saturated fat: 0g; Cholesterol: 0mg; Carbs: 13g; Fiber: 0g; Protein: 0g; Sodium: 1mg

1. In a medium saucepan over high heat, bring the water to a boil. Remove the pan from the heat and add the tea bags. Let the tea steep for 3 to 5 minutes. Remove and discard the tea bags, and let the tea cool to room temperature.

2. Stir in the frozen lemonade concentrate until blended.

3. Stir in the moonshine. Serve over ice.

HOW-TO TIP: To make sweetened Southern iced tea, prepare the tea as directed. After removing the tea bags, stir in ½ to 1 cup sugar, depending on the sweetness desired. Let cool.

VARIATION TIP: To make a nonalcoholic version of this recipe, substitute ½ cup lemon-lime soda for the moonshine.

SOUTHERN SANGRIA

| DF | GF | NF | V |

New Favorite | SERVES **8**

Sangria is, in my humble opinion, the best way to use a bottle of wine. It's also one of the best ways to use fruit. Our Southern version includes mint, partially because it's a popular addition to any Southern cocktail. The other reason is, well, our yard is full of mint. We planted one mint plant a long time ago, and it's become a good portion of our garden, thanks to its grass-like root system and ability to thrive in just about any situation. When we mow our yard, it smells like someone is making mojitos. It's certainly better than the smell of onion grass that permeates our neighborhood during the summer, but it has the peculiar effect of making me crave a glass of this Southern take on sangria, made with those famous Georgia peaches.

1 (750-milliliter) bottle of white wine
    or Moscato
1 cup unsweetened pineapple juice
½ cup freshly squeezed orange juice
¼ cup freshly squeezed lemon juice
¼ cup sugar
¾ cup lemon-lime soda
2 fresh (Georgia, preferably) peaches,
    peeled and chopped
¾ cup honeydew melon, chopped
4 fresh mint leaves

PREP TIME: 15 minutes, plus 2 hours chilling time

PER SERVING: Calories: 211; Total fat: 0g; Saturated fat: 0g; Cholesterol: 0mg; Carbs: 19g; Fiber: 1g; Protein: 1g; Sodium: 7mg

1. In a large pitcher, combine the wine, pineapple juice, orange juice, lemon juice, and sugar. Stir until the sugar dissolves. Refrigerate for 2 hours.

2. Just before serving, remove the sangria from the refrigerator and stir in the lemon-lime soda.

3. Add the peaches, melon, and mint leaves, and enjoy.

VARIATION TIP: To make this nonal-coholic, substitute 1 (750-milliliter) bottle of sparkling white grape juice for the white wine. Add freshly chopped pineapple and lemons instead of peaches and melon.

RUSSIAN TEA

Heirloom Recipe | MAKES **18** (8-OUNCE) SERVINGS

You can't write about Russian tea without writing about my Grandmother Wattenbarger. An accomplished home cook, she always has something going in a cast iron pan or in a casserole dish stowed in the oven. Her goal, it seems, is to make the entire family fat. *That's not an exaggeration.* One of the first things she said about my now-husband, after their initial meeting, was, "He's a little scrawny, ain't he?"

Although we love many of her recipes, none sticks out in my mind like Russian tea. This spiced tea appears only during the brief Southern winter, and Grandmother can never remember which of the grandkids actually like it. Since she often thinks I don't like it, sometimes all the tea is gone before I get there. Luckily, one winter, she finally deemed me worthy to receive the recipe for myself. Now, I can make it anytime I want.

1 quart water

1 cup freshly squeezed lemon juice

2 cinnamon sticks

1 tablespoon whole cloves

1 family-size iced tea bag, or 2 to 3 regular tea bags

1 (59-ounce) bottle orange juice

1 (46-ounce) bottle pineapple juice

1½ cups sugar, or to taste

PREP TIME: 25 minutes

PER SERVING: Calories: 146; Total fat: 0g; Saturated fat: 0g; Cholesterol: 0mg; Carbs: 36g; Fiber: 0g; Protein: 1g; Sodium: 5mg

1. In a large saucepan over high heat, combine the water, lemon juice, cinnamon sticks, and cloves. Bring to a rolling boil. Remove from the heat and add the tea bag(s). Cover the pan and let the tea steep for 10 minutes.

2. Strain the mixture into a large bowl or pitcher; discard the spices and tea bag(s).

3. Stir in the orange juice, pineapple juice, and sugar. Serve warm or over ice.

MAKE-AHEAD TIP: The tea can be made in advance and kept warm in a slow cooker on low heat. This can also be served chilled. Prepare as directed and freeze additional pineapple and orange juice in ice trays. Substitute these for ice cubes.

SOUTHERN FRIED KUDZU AND GARDEN ROSE TEA

'm sure most people haven't looked at a kudzu vine and thought, "Mmmm, dinner!" But not everyone is Brittany and Taylor. . . . We've had many cooking adventures on the wild side as children—from spicy salad food truck dreams to gourmet ramen noodles, nothing was off limits. One time, we even fried up a wonderful dish of kudzu. Yep, that vine you see clinging to almost everything in the South. *In our defense, we did first Google it to see if it was edible, but I digress.*

There's one particular memory that sticks with me. One hot summer afternoon, Brittany and I were dying of boredom. So we decided it was a fantastic idea to head to the backyard for ingredients. What better idea than to raid Pam's garden for our childhood cooking experiments? Without her permission—I'm sure—we went into the garden with a basket and a mission.

Suddenly, an idea formed. Rose tea! It sounded delicious and weird, which fit our main criteria. We came inside and started boiling the water with rose petals. I don't have a recipe to give you, which is probably best for everyone. After we finished steeping the tea and adding some sugar, we called in our usually unwilling test subject, Brittany's younger brother, Ashton.

Long story short, he did not enjoy the tea at first. Nor did he enjoy the tea later when his face puffed up like an angry blowfish. Brittany and I thought it was hilarious, which did not go over well with the rest of the family. Luckily, there was Benadryl on hand to serve as a post-tea salve.

If you plan to make this fragrant tea at home, please make sure no one in your party is allergic to this particular perennial flowering plant. Cheers!

—*Taylor Shook*
(BRITTANY'S CHILDHOOD FRIEND)

SPIKED PEPPERMINT HOT CHOCOLATE

GF | **NF** | **V**

Updated Classic | SERVES **4**

One of my bucket list items was attending Mardi Gras in Louisiana. When I was invited to a celebration in Shreveport, I was thrilled. The highlight was riding in the Mardi Gras parade and attending the VIP after-party. The day of the parade dawned, cold and rainy. We pulled on coats, hats, and scarves. I stuffed hand warmers in my pockets and foot warmers in my shoes. "So, how long does this parade last?" I asked, mistakenly thinking it was like the small-town parades in my hometown, with a span of 20 minutes. "The route takes about three hours," the driver told me.

I had a great time throwing beads and cups, but as the parade continued, I grew colder and colder. As soon as we parked, I ran for the after-party area. "What do you have that will warm me up?" I asked. "Whiskey," the bartender replied. I wrinkled my nose. "I don't like whiskey. Have you anything else?" She did: flavored liquor with coffee. I re-created this drink at home with hot chocolate.

2 cups whole milk

1 to 2 tablespoons sugar, depending on the variety of chocolate (use more sugar for bittersweet or dark chocolate and less for milk chocolate)

½ teaspoon vanilla extract

¼ teaspoon salt

6 ounces good quality chocolate, coarsely chopped (your choice of dark or milk)

¼ cup peppermint vodka

Whipped cream (optional)

1. In a medium saucepan over low heat, combine the milk, sugar, vanilla, and salt. Cook for 5 minutes, stirring constantly. Do not let the milk boil.

2. Put the chocolate in a medium bowl.

3. Pour the hot milk over the chocolate. Stir until the chocolate is melted.

4. Stir in the peppermint vodka.

5. Pour the hot chocolate into 4 cups and top with whipped cream (if using).

INGREDIENT TIP: In a hurry? Use 6 ounces good quality semisweet chocolate chips instead of chopping the chocolate bars.

PREP TIME: 15 minutes

COOK TIME: 5 minutes

PER SERVING: Calories: 346; Total fat: 17g; Saturated fat: 11g; Cholesterol: 22mg; Carbs: 34g; Fiber: 2g; Protein: 7g; Sodium: 230mg

VARIATION TIP: To make a nonalcoholic version, omit the vodka and add ¼ cup crushed peppermint candy to the chocolate mixture. Stir until dissolved.

DAIRY-FREE AND VEGAN OPTION: Use vanilla almond milk and vegan chocolate, and skip the whipped cream.

STRAWBERRY SMOOTHIE

| GF | NF | V |

New Favorite | SERVES **2**

When Brittany and her best friend, Taylor, decided they wanted to learn how to cook, I had just had my kitchen remodeled. I was so proud of the gleaming surfaces, the new appliances, and best of all, the new cabinets. I'd lovingly picked out the wood, found a design I liked, and had a local cabinetmaker custom build them.

This seemed like the perfect way to put my new kitchen to use. So I found this smoothie recipe and had them gather ingredients. "Now we put it in the blender and turn it on," I told them. About this time, I had to go outside to check on my son. I came back to find my new cabinets, top and bottom, oozing red liquid. The countertop was covered, and liquid dribbled down my dishwasher, pooling on the floor. "We forgot to put the lid on," they said. I threatened to *jerk a knot in their tails* if they did it again. They never did get knots jerked, so I suppose it was an idle threat. In the end, the taste of this smoothie was worth the mess. Using the dairy-free option means everyone can enjoy it.

1 banana, frozen
1 cup frozen strawberries
½ cup frozen pineapple chunks
1 cup frozen vanilla yogurt
¼ cup whole or 2% milk (optional)

PREP TIME: 5 minutes

PER SERVING: Calories: 185; Total fat: 2g; Saturated fat: 1g; Cholesterol: 5mg; Carbs: 43g; Fiber: 4g; Protein: 2g; Sodium: 32mg

1. In a blender, combine the banana, strawberries, and pineapple. Process *(with the lid on!)* for 5 seconds.

2. Add the frozen yogurt and milk (if using). Process until mixed. Serve immediately.

INGREDIENT TIP: It's easier to work with frozen bananas if you peel them and cut them into chunks before freezing.

VARIATION TIP: Substitute frozen peaches for the pineapple or frozen chocolate yogurt for the vanilla.

DAIRY-FREE AND VEGAN OPTION: Use coconut-based frozen yogurt and vanilla almond milk.

PEANUT BUTTER–CHOCOLATE SHAKE

GF | **V**

Updated Classic | SERVES **2**

I love chocolate and peanut butter, and my friends tease me about my slight obsession. Once, in our local church cookbook, I shared so many chocolate-peanut butter dessert recipes someone asked me, "Does your family eat anything besides peanut butter?" *The answer is yes, we do, but it's still my favorite.*

Each summer, the fast-food restaurant located about a mile from our house offers "half price after 8 shakes." Sometimes, we'd surprise the kids with a late-night trip for shakes. Since the menu was on his side of the car, Bryan would patiently read all the many flavors available. He rolled his eyes so hard I thought they'd pop out after he read the menu *twice* while I asked, "What was new again?" . . . and then ordered my usual peanut butter-chocolate milkshake.

This is our re-creation of that shake, and it's just as good as theirs.

2 cups chocolate ice cream

½ cup whole milk

½ cup peanut butter

1 tablespoon chocolate syrup, plus more for drizzling (optional)

½ teaspoon vanilla extract

Whipped cream, for topping (optional)

Maraschino cherries, for garnishing (optional)

PREP TIME: 5 minutes

PER SERVING: Calories: 609; Total fat: 46g; Saturated fat: 15g; Cholesterol: 46mg; Carbs: 34g; Fiber: 5g; Protein: 17g; Sodium: 356mg

DAIRY-FREE AND VEGAN OPTION: Use coconut ice cream and soy milk.

1. In a blender, combine the ice cream, milk, peanut butter, chocolate syrup, and vanilla. Blend for 10 to 20 seconds.

2. Drizzle additional chocolate syrup down the inside of a glass (if desired), and pour in the shake.

3. Top with whipped cream and a cherry (if using).

INGREDIENT TIP: Like to add different candies to your milkshake? Purchase marked-down chocolate candy after the holiday, place it in an airtight freezer bag, and freeze for up to 18 months. You'll always have candy available!

VARIATION TIP: Want to make this a candy milkshake? Add a crumbled peanut butter cup.

MENUS *for* HOLIDAYS *&* SPECIAL OCCASIONS

HOLIDAYS

EASTER

Strawberry Smoothie (page 182)

Ambrosia (page 40)

Blue Cheese and Bacon Deviled Eggs
(page 31)

Newfangled Creamed Corn (page 52)

Old-Fashioned Glazed Ham (page 138)

Chocolate Pie with Coconut Crust
(page 150)

MOTHER'S DAY BRUNCH

Pineapple-Orange Mimosas (page 173)

Bacon Pimento Cheese (page 30)

Ham Breakfast Casserole (page 22)

Baked Chicken Salad (page 85)

Shrimp Remoulade (page 116)

Bacon and Tomato Pie (page 130)

Pecan Pie Tarts (page 156)

INDEPENDENCE DAY

Southern Sangria (page 177)

Watermelon Salsa (page 39)

Fried Green Tomatoes with Garlic Aioli
(page 54)

Honey Lemon Grilled Chicken (page 102)

Honey Grilled Peaches (page 33)

Lemon Ice (page 174)

THANKSGIVING

Russian Tea (page 178)

Cranberry Muffins (page 16)

Corn and Tomato Skillet (page 59)

Fried Green Tomatoes with Garlic Aioli
(page 54)

Chicken and Corn Bread Dressing
(page 86)

Sweet Potato Pie with Pecan Topping
(page 160)

CHRISTMAS

Russian Tea (page 178)

Ambrosia (page 40)

Wilted Lettuce Salad (page 46)

Sweet Potato Muffins (page 18)

Blue Cheese and Bacon Deviled Eggs (page 31)

Old-Fashioned Glazed Ham (page 138)

Peanut Butter Sheet Cake (page 152)

SPECIAL OCCASIONS

KIDS' BIRTHDAY

Peanut Butter–Chocolate Shake (page 183)

Corn Relish (page 37), served with tortilla chips

Cheesy Baked Chicken Strips (page 92)

Herbed Skillet Potatoes (page 57)

Classic Tea Cakes (page 164)

COMPANY DINNER

Updated Arnold Palmer (page 176)

Angel Biscuits with Sausage Gravy (page 10)

Wilted Lettuce Salad (page 46)

Easy Marinated Herbed Cauliflower and Chickpeas (page 58)

Chicken in Lemon Cream Sauce (page 84)

Fresh Apple Cake (page 154)

SUNDAY SUPPER

Peachy Slush Cooler (page 175)

Angel Biscuits with Sausage Gravy (page 10)

Squash Puppies (page 14)

Oven-Fried Cornmeal Pecan Catfish with Lemon Thyme Mayonnaise (page 108)

Slow Cooker Apple Cobbler (page 166)

MEAT AND THREE

Strawberry Lemonade Iced Tea (page 172)

Broccoli Corn Bread (page 13)

Herbed Skillet Potatoes (page 57)

Cheesy Squash (page 56)

Freezer Slaw (page 48)

Chicken Fried Steak with Gravy (page 146)

Buttermilk Pie (page 158)

TAILGATING PARTY

Spiked Peppermint Hot Chocolate (page 180)

Black Bean Dip (page 32)

Vidalia Onion Dip (page 36)

Freezer Slaw (page 48)

Honey Barbecue Wings with Peach Sweet 'n' Sour Sauce (page 98)

Slow-Cooked Barbecue Pork (page 140)

My Dad's Favorite Chili (page 76)

Sand Tarts (page 168)

GLOSSARY of SOUTHERN SAYINGS

"BLESS YOUR HEART."

A common phrase with many meanings. It can be used for sympathy, as in, "And then that goat ate every one of her roses. Bless her heart." It is also used sarcastically as an insult. "You ate the entire pie? Well, bless your heart!"

"ABOUT TO POP."

Very full. "I ate so much I'm about to pop!"

"DRY AS A BONE."

Very thirsty. "Give me some of that strawberry lemonade tea. I'm dry as a bone."

"LIVING HIGH ON THE HOG."

Living the good life. "They bought a new home, new car, and put in a pool. They're living high on the hog."

"'TIL THE COWS COME HOME."

Meaning a long time. "You are staying right here until the cows come home!"

"GIVE ME SOME SUGAR."

Kiss me. "Aw. I haven't seen you in forever! Give me some sugar."

"FISH OR CUT BAIT."

Help or move out of the way. "I need some help moving this piano. Are you going to fish or cut bait?"

"TWO PEAS IN A POD."

Almost identical. "Those two are just alike. They're like two peas in a pod."

"THAT REALLY STIRS MY STEW."

To make someone angry. "I can't believe she did that. That really stirs my stew."

"FLY THE COOP."

To escape or flee. "I was trying to explain this recipe to him, and he flew the coop."

"SLOW AS MOLASSES."

Very slow. "She's slow as molasses when she's getting ready to leave."

"FINER THAN FROG HAIR."

Very good. "This recipe is finer than frog hair."

"GET GLAD IN THE SAME BRITCHES YOU GOT MAD IN."

Get over it. "Well, you can just get glad in the same britches you got mad in."

"OVER YONDER."

Anything at a distance. "Can you get the knife? I set it down over yonder."

"FULL AS A TICK."

Very full. "I ate so much I am full as a tick."

"GET YOUR FEATHERS RUFFLED."

To be mad. "Aw, that's nothing to get your feathers ruffled about."

"FLY OFF THE HANDLE."

To be angry. "And then he just flew off the handle."

"BEATIN' AROUND THE BUSH."

Talking about something without getting to the point. "Stop beatin' around the bush and tell me what happened."

"IF IT HAD BEEN A SNAKE, IT WOULD HAVE BIT YOU."

Something that is in plain sight. "You didn't see the ketchup in the fridge? It's right here. If it had been a snake, it would have bit you."

"HOLD YOUR HORSES."

Wait a minute. "I'll make dinner as soon as I finish folding laundry. Hold your horses."

MEASUREMENT CONVERSIONS

VOLUME EQUIVALENTS (LIQUID)

US STANDARD	US STANDARD (OUNCES)	METRIC (APPROXIMATE)
2 tablespoons	1 fl. oz.	30 mL
¼ cup	2 fl. oz.	60 mL
½ cup	4 fl. oz.	120 mL
1 cup	8 fl. oz.	240 mL
1½ cups	12 fl. oz.	355 mL
2 cups or 1 pint	16 fl. oz.	475 mL
4 cups or 1 quart	32 fl. oz.	1 L
1 gallon	128 fl. oz.	4 L

VOLUME EQUIVALENTS (DRY)

US STANDARD	METRIC (APPROXIMATE)
⅛ teaspoon	0.5 mL
¼ teaspoon	1 mL
½ teaspoon	2 mL
¾ teaspoon	4 mL
1 teaspoon	5 mL
1 tablespoon	15 mL
¼ cup	59 mL
⅓ cup	79 mL
½ cup	118 mL
⅔ cup	156 mL
¾ cup	177 mL
1 cup	235 mL
2 cups or 1 pint	475 mL
3 cups	700 mL
4 cups or 1 quart	1 L

OVEN TEMPERATURES

FAHRENHEIT (F)	CELSIUS (C) (APPROXIMATE)
250°F	120°C
300°F	150°C
325°F	165°C
350°F	180°C
375°F	190°C
400°F	200°C
425°F	220°C
450°F	230°C

WEIGHT EQUIVALENTS

US STANDARD	METRIC (APPROXIMATE)
½ ounce	15 g
1 ounce	30 g
2 ounces	60 g
4 ounces	115 g
8 ounces	225 g
12 ounces	340 g
16 ounces or 1 pound	455 g

RECIPE INDEX

INDEX

ACKNOWLEDGMENTS

WE'D LIKE TO THANK our publisher, Rockridge Press/Callisto Media, for making our dream a reality. Thanks to the editorial staff—Vanessa Putt and Elizabeth Castoria—for discovering our recipes and our unusual sense of humor; Salwa Jabado, for patiently guiding us and answering all our questions; Mary Cassells, for making our manuscript publisher worthy; and the design team for the mouthwatering photography.

Thanks to Mary Veazey, Cristal Whitlock, and Denise Yates for recipe contributions, and Taylor Shook for sharing her cooking memories with us.

Pam would like to thank the following: my husband, Bryan, for being my biggest supporter and encouraging me to follow my dreams; my son, Ashton Wattenbarger, and my son-in-law, Justin Race, for making dinner when I was too busy to cook; Barb Webb, for keeping me focused on my goals; and all of my family and friends for their encouragement over the years.

Brittany would like to thank the following: my wonderful husband and best friend, Justin Race, and my friend, Jen Allgayer, for watching the baby so I could write. A special thanks to my best friend and platonic soulmate, Taylor Shook, for sparking my love of cooking and for always eating what I cooked, even when it was bad. Thanks also to Paul and Leslie Spell of Humble Heart Farms, for igniting my passion for supporting local farms and businesses. Finally, I couldn't have done this without the rest of my family and friends, who always encourage and inspire me.

ABOUT *the* AUTHORS

PAM WATTENBARGER wants to live in a world where calories don't count, desserts are enjoyed at every meal, and family meals are an everyday occurrence. As a native Southerner, with family members living in different parts of the South since 1678, she's been influenced by home-style Southern cooking all her life. When she's not baking or cooking, you can find her traveling, gardening, and wrangling sheep or her grandchild. Connect with Pam and learn more about her traditional Southern dishes with allergy-friendly adaptions at her website, SimplySouthernMom.com or her new travel and recipe site, Exploravore.com.

BRITTANY WATTENBARGER has never met a biscuit she didn't like. Having grown up with a family that shows love through food, her life was changed when she developed celiac disease and her daughter was born with a milk allergy. She's spent the past few years re-creating her child-hood favorites, minus the allergens. When she's not picnicking by a creek or hosting dinner parties, she can usually be found in her hammock with a good book and a glass of sweet tea.

CPSIA information can be obtained
at www.ICGtesting.com
Printed in the USA
BVHW05s1745220818
525188BV00002B/2/P

9 781641 521734